REASON TO BELIEVE

RICHARD L. PURTILL

REASON TO BELIEVE

Why Faith Makes Sense

IGNATIUS PRESS   SAN FRANCISCO

Cover art: *Incredulity of Saint Thomas* by Caravaggio
Scala/Art Resource, New York

Cover design by Riz Boncan Marsella

Published in 2009 by Ignatius Press
ISBN 978-1-58617-088-2
Library of Congress Control Number 2008926718
Printed in the United States of America ∞

To PAUL MAGNANO
Priest, Philosopher, Friend

and

to LILIA CASTLE
Teacher, Philosopher, Friend

Contents

Preface to the New Edition

Reason to Believe[1] was the third of my twenty-odd books and the first on philosophy of religion. It was followed by *Thinking about Religion* and *C. S. Lewis' Case for the Christian Faith*.[2] The original publication of *Reason to Believe* led to invitations to lecture at many universities, from Rhode Island to California, and to many lasting friendships with people interested in the philosophy of religion, both philosophers and nonphilosophers, clerics and laymen. I pursued my interest in philosophy of religion in my later career, which I combined with an interest in logic, ethics, and metaphysics.

Many of my later papers in philosophy of religion were on rather technical points, of interest only to professional philosophers. For this second edition, I have chosen to add a couple of related essays (see the appendixes) that I think illuminate my later thought on the subject. While I would still stand behind everything in *Reason to Believe*, the first essay provides a close examination of the idea of redemption in Christianity, and the second essay details some early influences on my thought and how they caused me to think of some of the recent history of the Church.

The first of these essays is "Justice, Mercy, and Atonement", an earlier version of which was read at Notre Dame University. The second, "Chesterton, the Wards, the Sheeds,

---

[1] *Reason to Believe*, 1st ed. (Grand Rapids, Mich.: Eerdmans, 1974).

[2] *Thinking about Religion* (Englewood Cliffs, N.J.: Prentice Hall, 1978); *C. S. Lewis' Case for the Christian Faith* (San Francisco: Harper, 1981; San Francisco: Ignatius Press, 2004).

and the Catholic Revival", was read at Seattle University and gives some idea of how my interest was first aroused in philosophy of religion and in conveying it to nonphilosophers. I did a similar thing in the second edition of *Lord of the Elves and Eldils: Fantasy and Philosophy in C. S. Lewis and J. R. R. Tolkien*,[3] adding two extra essays to the main book.

Over the years, I have received a number of appreciative comments on *Reason to Believe*. This edition, which includes new references to current editions of books cited, as well as a bibliography for further reading, will, I hope, get the same reaction from new readers as the original edition did.

—Richard Purtill
Bellingham, Washington

[3] *Lord of the Elves and Eldils: Fantasy and Philosophy in C. S. Lewis and J. R. R. Tolkien* (Grand Rapids, Mich.: Zondervan, 1974; 2nd ed., San Francisco: Ignatius Press, 2006).

Introduction

This is a book about philosophy of religion. Since *philosophy* and *religion* are both words of many meanings, I will begin by trying to clarify the two terms.

Philosophy, as it is understood by most contemporary philosophers, has the following characteristics.

1. An effort is made to state the point under discussion as clearly and understandably as possible. Thus a concept may be defined or explained, various possible interpretations of a thesis or statement may be discussed, an argument may be laid out formally or informally, and the relation of its premises to its conclusion discussed. Philosophers characteristically ask, "What do you mean?"

2. An effort is made to examine the point under discussion critically. Thus assumptions may be brought out into the open and examined, possible objections to a thesis may be stated as fairly as possible, and counterarguments may be invented or drawn from the arguments of opponents. Philosophers characteristically ask, "What are the objections?"

3. An effort is made to decide questions on the basis of arguments. Arguments for a thesis may be shown to be valid and their premises true. Counterarguments may be refuted or shown to be irrelevant. Definite conclusions may be reached, or it may be concluded that there is no conclusive argument for or against a position. Philosophers characteristically ask, "How can you show that?"

The above concerns are characteristic of philosophical *method*. When applied to trivial or specialized subject matter, philosophical method may not lead to philosophy in the full sense. Thus we must add to the above list something about subject matter.

4. The subject matter of philosophy can be roughly divided into logic and epistemology, which investigate the grounds of our knowledge; ethics, political philosophy, and aesthetics, which investigate questions of value; and metaphysics, which investigates questions about man, the universe, and God. Typical philosophical questions are, "Do we know anything?" "Do we have free will?" "Does God exist?" "Is there an objective standard of morality?" Notice that dogmatic answers to such questions do not constitute philosophy. The answers must be supported by means of the philosophical method described above.

These four characteristics can be observed in the work of the great philosophers of the West (for example, Plato, Aristotle, Aquinas, Scotus, Hume, Berkeley, Descartes, Spinoza, Kant, Hegel, Mill, Peirce, Moore, and Wittgenstein), while it is not certain that they can be observed in any Eastern philosopher. There are also some philosophers in the Western tradition to whom these criteria do not clearly apply (for example, Nietzsche and Schopenhauer). Thus the sort of philosophy we have described is sometimes called *analytic philosophy* rather than simply *philosophy*. It should be understood, however, that analytic philosophy thus understood is a very broad term and is intended to apply to the whole history of philosophy.

Religion can be defined so widely as to mean whatever a man is deeply concerned about, but it is more useful to restrict the term to its primary meaning of "belief in a divine or superhuman power or powers, to be obeyed and wor-shiped as the creator(s) and ruler(s) of the universe". As this definition suggests, religion can be *monotheistic*, holding belief in one God, or *polytheistic*, holding belief in more than one God. There is also the view called *pantheism*, which holds that in some sense everything is divine or shares in divinity. There are two main nonreligious views: *agnosti-cism*, which holds that we do not know that any religious view is true, and *atheism*, which holds that we know that every religious view is false. We can, of course, distinguish various kinds of pantheism and panentheism (God *is* the world vs. God includes the world) and varieties of agnos-ticism (we *cannot* know vs. we do not as a matter of fact know).

Most readers of this book will not regard polytheism in its various forms as a serious possibility, though some may be tempted by the view that there are two "Gods", a good God and an evil "God". This view, which is called *dualism*, is suggested by the existence of evil in the world, and it will be discussed later in connection with the problem of evil. A few people today are impressed by some form of pantheism, especially as it appears in one of the Eastern religions. We will discuss pantheism later in connection with ideas and arguments about the existence and nature of God.

Most people in the Western world, however, will have been influenced in their religious views by traditional Chris-tian monotheistic religion. Some may agree with this reli-gious tradition, while others may disagree; still others may partly agree and partly disagree. But most people brought up in this country or in countries of similar history and tradition will have formed their ideas about religion on the basis of the Christian religious tradition. For this reason, it seems appropriate to concentrate most of our attention on attacks on and defenses of monotheism as understood by Christians. Of course, Christians differ among themselves in their views about God, but it seems reasonable to begin with what might be called the traditional Christian idea of God as the Creator of the world, all-powerful, all-knowing, perfectly good, able to interfere miraculously with the course of nature, and able to reward or punish human souls for deeds done before their death. Whether this traditional account must be abandoned or seriously modified in the face of criticism is one of the main questions we will consider.

Traditionally, it has been thought that there were two ways of getting to know about God: the unaided efforts of our own minds, and some form of revelation to man from God. Philosophy is obviously relevant to efforts to obtain information about God by our own thinking, but it can also ask questions about the meaning and justification of statements that are claimed to be revelations from God. These two enterprises—the attempt to find answers to questions about God by thinking and argument, and the attempt to criticize rationally alleged revelations—are main concerns of the philosophy of religion.

It may be worthwhile to separate carefully philosophy of religion, so understood, from related enterprises. *Theology* accepts some body of revelation as a starting point and attempts to use reason to understand the revelation, draw out its consequences, and systematically relate its elements. *Apologetics* is the effort to defend some religious revelation against criticism, using arguments of various kinds, not only philosophical but historical and sometimes scientific. It is thus more restricted than philosophy of religion in its purposes and less restricted in the kind of arguments it uses. Philosophy of religion differs from theology by not accepting revelation as a starting point and from apologetics by "following the question wherever it leads" rather than defending some view against attacks.

Of course, a given philosopher of religion may come to the conclusion that a certain religious tradition is true and ought to be accepted. He may then use arguments very much like the theologian's or the apologist's to convince others of what he has become convinced. But this is because he has become convinced by a kind of inquiry that begins without commitment to the truth of a given view. The philosopher of religion is thus, in theory at least, like a judge, who begins hearing a case without having decided the question before him. The apologist, and to some extent the theologian, is more like the lawyer who pleads one side of the case.

In practice, of course, many philosophers of religion have made up their minds on one side or the other of the question. But in discussing the problems of philosophy of religion, they will make every effort to present both sides as fully and fairly as possible. They will act as philosophers, not as advocates. They will seek to convince by presenting the evidence fairly, not to persuade by presenting only one side of the case. Someone who does not act in this way has ceased to function as a philosopher of religion and has become an apologist or an "antiapologist", an advocate of the antireligious side.

Until fairly recently, many philosophers of religion believed they could present both sides fairly only by carefully concealing their own points of view and their own conclusions about the questions at issue. This was always somewhat unrealistic, and with the emphasis on honesty and commitment in recent years it is no longer seen as desirable by many philosophers. They believe it is fairer and more honest to make clear on what side of a question the philosopher's own convictions lie and then to present the arguments pro and con. If students were ever inclined docilely to accept their teachers' ideas without critical examination, they are certainly not so inclined now.

My own convictions on the matters discussed in this book are quite clear-cut. I am a professional philosopher, and I consider myself to be working within the "analytic" tradition of modern philosophy, a tradition influenced by the logical positivists, by Wittgenstein, and by the "Oxford" or "ordinary language" school of Austin and Ryle. Like a number of such philosophers, a number that includes some of the most able representatives of the tradition, I am also a Christian. I have published a number of technical articles and books having to do with metaphysics, epistemology, and philosophy of science, as well as four books on logic. I find no contradiction between analytic philosophy and traditional Christianity, between logic and the love of God. It is the theme of this book that no such opposition exists and that clear and logical thinking leads us not in the direction of unbelief, not in the direction of "liberal" reinterpretations of Christianity, but rather leads us back to traditional Christian answers to the problems that confront us. Logic alone cannot lead us all the way to Christian belief. But like Dante's Virgil, it is an incomparable guide so far as it goes. And like Dante, I believe that if we go this far with honesty and good will, help will be given to us to finish the journey.

As you will see from the Contents, my strategy in this book is to consider the negative side first and answer common objections to religious belief. In the second part of the book, I consider the positive arguments in favor of Christian belief, which might not gain a hearing until some answer had been given to the objection. In the third part, I turn to certain puzzles about the Christian revelation, both to answer objections and to give a fuller understanding that can provide grounds for belief. To answer objections and to give grounds for belief will not necessarily lead to religious commitment, but it is an important first step toward such commitment.

One final point: any vigorous argument that comes to definite conclusions is bound to seem one-sided at times, and any attempt to cover a number of important issues in a limited space is bound to simplify and to ignore some ambiguities and qualifications. Sometimes in trying to be clear and brief, this book may sound dogmatic. Let us make it clear then that many sincere and intelligent people do have what seem to them to be good reasons for agnosticism or atheism. Not every objection to theism can be considered in a single book, and many people may believe that they have satisfactory replies to some of the arguments given in what follows. Thus a single book, a single class, a single teacher, may be only the start of a long dialogue, with oneself and with others. But reason, like every good thing, leads us ultimately to God. The better we reason, the nearer we come to Truth.

PART I

OBJECTIONS

I

The Accusation of Nonsense

The idea that "science" has disproved traditional religious ideas can mean one of two things. It can mean that some specific scientific discovery or discoveries has disproved some specific traditional doctrine or doctrines. This claim has sometimes been made, but there are not many plausible candidates for such a discovery. Rightly understood, the existence of God, the immortality of the soul, and other key ideas of traditional religion can be neither proved nor disproved by experiment or observation. The method of science is the statement of clear and exact hypotheses, often in mathematical form; the deduction of precise consequences from such hypotheses; and the testing of these consequences by controlled observation. This method is not applicable to philosophical questions. As Socrates pointed out long ago, questions that can be settled by calculation or observation are not those about which philosophical disputes arise.

To some, this may seem an evasion. They have in the back of their minds the ideal that all "real" or "meaningful" questions *should* be questions that can be settled by the methods of science or mathematics. This, however, is not a scientific theory or discovery but a philosophical theory. It is, in fact, the philosophical theory known as *logical positivism*. This theory seems plausible because of its confusion with a commonsense standard of meaningfulness. We ordinarily think that if a statement is meaningful then there must be some way of deciding whether it is true or false. Someone who claims to have made a meaningful statement but cannot tell us what would count for or against the truth of that statement is rightly regarded with suspicion. What the logical positivist does is to take this commonsense position and modify it in an apparently minor way. He inserts the requirement that a meaningful statement must be provable or disprovable only in certain ways—roughly speaking, by the methods of empirical science or by the methods of mathematics. In fact, it turns out that when we try to make this more specific, we find there is no way to rule out metaphysical hypotheses about the existence of God and the soul without at the same time ruling out scientific hypotheses about things like subatomic particles, which cannot be directly observed.

A subatomic particle, for example, especially one such as a neutrino, which has no charge and no mass when at rest, cannot be directly observed. If we are to admit its existence, we can do so only because of its effect on other things. Of course, our reasons for believing in the existence of neutrinos are quite different from our reasons for believing in the existence of God or the soul. But if we admit indirect arguments for the existence of neutrinos from the behavior of observable material objects, no amount of ingenuity has so far succeeded in logically ruling out the possibility of arguments for God or the soul on the basis of the behavior of observable objects.

But there is a more serious objection to logical positivism. Its own basic principle—that a meaningful statement must be provable or disprovable by the methods of science or mathematics—cannot itself be proved or disproved by the methods of science or mathematics. Thus the principle is meaningless by the standard it itself lays down and is thus self-refuting.

The positivists exerted great ingenuity in trying to justify their principle in some plausible way—as an analysis of what we ordinarily mean by "meaningful", as a necessary presupposition of science, as a recommendation rather than a statement, and so on. But all these attempts leave the door open for philosophy, and therefore for ethics and metaphysics, and therefore ultimately for religion. If we are to analyze meanings of words in ordinary use, some of such analyses may favor religious or metaphysical ideas (as an analysis of our ordinary language about mind, for example, arguably does). If we are to examine presuppositions, even science may have presuppositions that accord with religion—for example, a presupposition that the universe is intelligible and orderly. If the positivist's principle is merely a recommendation as to how we should use language, believers may find reasons for rejecting the recommendation or may have recommendations of their own.

Thus positivism, as an attempt to shortcut the discussion of philosophical and religious questions by dismissing certain statements as meaningless, is a failure. For modern philosophy it was an interesting and even a productive failure, but hardly any philosopher would not deny that it *was* a failure.

A somewhat more subtle attack on the credibility of religion came from the later work of the influential modern philosopher Ludwig Wittgenstein. His earlier work had shared the assumptions of the logical positivists and stimulated some of their thinking. But he became dissatisfied with positivism and began to look at ordinary language rather than at science in his attempt to solve philosophical problems. He arrived at the view that a great many philosophical problems arise from trying to use ordinary language in inappropriate ways and that the business of philosophy is to "cure" the confusions that arise in this way. This view, sometimes called *therapeutic positivism*, is still held by some followers of Wittgenstein, though it has been extensively criticized and rejected by many contemporary philosophers.

Given Wittgenstein's objections to "inappropriate" uses of ordinary language, the objections to religious belief developed by some philosophers influenced by Wittgenstein could perhaps be guessed. When we apply words like *good* or *wise* or *powerful* to God, we apply terms we have learned in everyday contexts to a being completely beyond our experience. Wittgensteinians have suggested that when we use such words in this way, they are not meaningful. Similarly, all our experience of persons has been of "embodied" persons, and our language about persons was learned from such cases. So Wittgensteinians have argued that the very concept of a disembodied person—a soul without a body—is meaningless and that we can say nothing meaningful about such a being.

Wittgensteinians, partly because of Wittgenstein's ideas about the nature of philosophy, have not clearly stated their standard or criterion of meaningfulness. But insofar as we can reconstruct such a standard from their arguments, it seems to be open to objections, some of which are parallel to those that were fatal to the positivist principle.

The Wittgensteinian criterion of meaningfulness rests on making a close connection between meaning and use. We can understand a word or sentence only by understanding its use in language, said Wittgenstein. From this it seems to follow that if we use words or sentences in ways very different from their ordinary use in language, we may not be making sense.

But when we try to state this more precisely, we find that it falls to pieces. What is the ordinary use, and how different must a use be from the ordinary use before it becomes nonsense? What if it is argued that the use of *good* as applied to God, or *happy* as applied to disembodied souls, *is* an ordinary use?

Furthermore, Wittgenstein's idea of meaningfulness, or at least that of some of his followers, seems to rest on an absurdly oversimplified idea of how we learn and use language. Norman Malcolm, for example, is generally recognized as one of Wittgenstein's foremost followers and interpreters (although it is only fair to say that other Wittgensteinians violently reject Malcolm's interpretations). In his book *Dreaming*,[1] Malcolm argues that it is absurd to apply concepts such as fearing, judging, liking, etc., to dream experiences. For, argues Malcolm, if a concept is to be meaningful, it must be possible to apply it correctly; and if it is possible to apply it correctly, it must be possible to apply it incorrectly. But correct and incorrect application of concepts can be learned only by being in a situation where someone can observe your use of a concept and correct you if you use it incorrectly. Since dreams, as usually conceived, are necessarily private experiences that no one can share with you, it follows that you can never be in a situation where someone is in a position to observe your use of a concept such as "judging in a dream", "fearing in a dream", etc., and to correct your misuses. Thus such concepts are meaningless. Malcolm seems to conclude, in fact, that we can never really have such experiences as dreams

[1] *Dreaming* (London: Routledge and Kegan Paul, 1959).

are usually thought to be—completely private and completely insulated from the outside world. Dreams, for Malcolm, become essentially false memories; on awaking we seem to remember judging, fearing, walking, but these supposed memories correspond to no real experiences.

This bizarre conclusion, which directly contradicts what most people would say about their own experience of dreams, is evidently arrived at on the basis of a requirement that to learn a concept properly we must be able to apply it and to receive correction on our application of it *at the time we are having the experience.* We can easily think of experiences (for example, excruciating pain or complete paralysis) in which this requirement seems ridiculous, for one reason or another. But perhaps Malcolm can modify his requirement in this way: the experience must be such that someone else *can* observe us having the experience and at some later time can correct our application of a concept to that experience. This amounts to a ruling out of essentially private experiences (like dreams) as "real" experiences. Since concepts cannot be meaningfully applied to such experiences, we cannot meaningfully talk about them.

But this requirement in either form is vastly implausible. It is not self-refuting, and in this it is unlike the positivist's principle. But there seems no good reason to adopt such a stringent principle, and one that has such odd consequences. For example, most people have had dreams in which they are able to float or fly through the air. This is quite a recognizable sensation and any two people who have had this dream can compare notes and be quite sure that they have had the same experience in their dreams. But on Malcolm's theory this is impossible, since in the nature of the case the two cannot observe each other having the experience. Furthermore, since many of our emotions, daydreams, and thoughts *seem* to be unobservable by outside observers, either they also must be rejected as genuine experiences or their apparent privacy must be denied. Many Wittgensteinians have taken the second course, leading them to a philosophical position akin to behaviorism. But the denial that we have interior states and the denial that these states are in a certain sense inaccessible to others are both so implausible that any philosophical theory that purports to prove such conclusions must be mistaken. It must rest on premises less certain than our certainty that we have private experiences.

Further difficulties in the Wittgensteinian theory of meaningfulness can be seen when we reflect on the way in which we actually acquire concepts. Consider, for example, the way we in fact learn to use any reasonably complex and abstract concept, for example, "power", "prestige", or "privacy". Consider the way words are metaphorically extended from their original use, the way concepts learned in one context can be applied in a completely new context. With all this in mind, we can see that the picture that is apparently back of the Wittgensteinian theory is one that applies only to some very simple kinds of concept learning. Little Johnny and his father in the presence of a cat, with Father saying, "No, Johnny, that's a kitty, not a doggie", seems to be the paradigm they have in mind. But very little language learning is really like that.

If the Wittgensteinians say that observability in principle by a person other than the concept user is a sine qua non for meaningful use of concepts, there seems to be no reason to accept this requirement. The requirement is not self-evident, and so far as I can see, the Wittgensteinians have no argument to support it.

There is also a difficulty like the difficulty about the positivist's principle: how far is observability of experiences "in principle" to be stretched? If we stretch it far enough, we let in experiences the Wittgensteinians wish to rule out; if we resist stretching it, we may rule out experiences anyone would wish to admit.

We must conclude, then, that the Wittgensteinian theory of meaning runs into such serious difficulties that its use to criticize religious concepts need not worry us much.

The final criticism of religious belief from the point of view of contemporary philosophy that we shall consider is a modification of the positivist's principle that has been urged by some "Oxford" or "ordinary language" philosophers. They argue that a belief that is consistent with any observable state of affairs is empty or meaningless. Any meaningful statement excludes something, rules out some state of affairs. If a thing is green, it is not red, blue, or purple; if a thing is colored, it is not colorless; and so on. A theory that is unfalsifiable, that cannot be disproved by any possible turn of events, can only be a tautology, on the order of "Either it is raining or it is not raining", or else it is an empty statement that says nothing. Suppose, for example, two people disagree about whether a garden, which shows some signs of being taken care of, is being tended by a gardener. They watch and see no gardener. The person who believes there is a gardener suggests that the gardener is invisible. They set trip wires and traps—no result. The believer suggests that the gardener is intangible, too. At some point the sceptical member of the pair can ask how an invisible, intangible, undetectable gardener is different from no gardener at all.

These philosophers argue that Christian beliefs—for example, the belief that God is loving or good—are in a similar position. Doesn't the goodness of God mean that he will take care of us? But all kinds of disasters occur to us. Perhaps these are in some way means to a greater good. But suppose things get worse and worse. Surely, it is argued, at some point we might as well say that God hates us, as that he loves us. Unless a belief can be disproved by some state of affairs, it is meaningless. But, they argue, the Christian is committed to belief in God "no matter what". Thus, he will allow nothing as disproving his beliefs, and so his belief is empty or nonsensical.

A complete answer to this objection would require an analysis of religious belief, which we shall attempt later. A short answer that can be given at this point is that the objection rests on a confusion. The religious believer is told to expect suffering for himself and for others in this life. Keeping his faith despite this suffering is, he knows, part of his task. He expects vindication not in this life but after death. The idea that the good man should expect to be plentifully rewarded with material goods, security, and settled happiness in this life was to some extent an Old Testament idea, although the book of Job is a powerful rebuke to this expectation. Some Christians, and some groups of Christians, seem to have had such an expectation, but it is a Christian heresy rather than a part of Christian belief. Certainly Christ's own words would lead his followers to expect trials and suffering.

Thus, if the argument is, "If Christianity is true, good Christians should be prosperous, secure, and content, but they are not, so Christianity is false", the first premise would simply be denied by most Christians. But the argument we are speaking of is not so simple. Rather, the argument is: "You say that God is good and loves men. But apparently this 'love' is compatible with inflicting great sufferings on those he 'loves', sufferings no good human being would inflict on those he loves. So apparently God's 'goodness' and 'love' mean nothing, or they mean something entirely different from what goodness and love mean when we talk about human beings."

Again, there is a long answer, which we will consider in our chapter on the problem of evil, and a short answer, which we can give now. The short answer is that, on the Christian view, great suffering in this life has a purpose—to create characters of a certain sort. What *would* be inconsistent with Christian beliefs in God's love and goodness would be a failure of their expectations about life after death—to take an extreme example, the eternal punishment of all good men, and eternal reward for all bad men. A less dramatic example would simply be annihilation for the souls of all, good or bad, at death.

To those who make the objection we are discussing, this seems an evasion. "The proof or disproof of your ideas lies comfortably beyond immediate verification", they would say. But of course, the same may be said about any statement about the future. Unless there is some special difficulty about life after death, the accusation of meaninglessness because of unfalsifiability must be abandoned. Some defenders of the objection we are considering then fall back on positivist or Wittgensteinian objections to the concept of life after death. But as we have seen, these objections are open to serious and probably fatal counterobjections.

One further line of argument must be examined on this point. Recently some analytic philosophers have produced a new argument against the meaningfulness of survival after death, which can be stated as follows:

The idea of disembodied survival is meaningless, for there can be no standard by which we could identify a disembodied soul and say that it was the soul of a given person who had died. The only possible standards for identifying someone as the same person are bodily continuity and memory. But memory is not an independent criterion. It depends on bodily continuity. Since bodily continuity is ruled out by the very hypothesis in disembodied survival, no possible standard remains.

Let us expand this argument somewhat. It is of course true that our normal way of reidentifying someone after a period of time is bodily continuity. Even if he has lost his memory or changed his habits or his character, if the body we now encounter can be traced back to the body we previously encountered, we regard him as the same person. It is also true that supposed memories can be mistaken and that our ordinary ways of deciding whether a memory is true or false include checking on whether the body of the person making a memory claim was in a place where and at a time when the experiences alleged to be remembered occurred. If you claim to remember meeting me at the coronation of Queen Elizabeth II but your body was not in England when the coronation occurred, we would reject your claimed memory, no matter how detailed and circumstantial it was. Thus, memory is not an independent criterion but is subordinate to bodily continuity.

Now, this argument is a very curious one. From a few commonplace observations about the way we in fact reidentify persons in everyday life, the consequence is drawn that a belief held for most of the history of the world by most of the people in the world is not only false, but meaningless!

It can be noticed that the argument is in the form of a dilemma. As with most dilemma arguments, we can deny that the alternatives posed are exhaustive ("going between the horns" of this dilemma), or we can accept one of the alternatives despite the apparent difficulties ("grasping one horn" of the dilemma). Or we can do both. Let us explore the first possibility.

The first thing to consider is that there may be some standard of personal identity other than bodily continuity and memory. An obvious choice is personality or character, in the wide sense. Consider some strongly marked personality, such as that of Dr. Samuel Johnson. His character undergoes important changes. At one time he is a young man, at another an old one. He is converted from an immoral life to a devout one; he changes some of his opinions and habits. But all of his actions are "characteristic" in a certain sense; they hang together. Many of his actions and sayings are "characteristic" in that while they are not predictable beforehand, once said or done they can be seen to fit into his character. Arguably, each person has this sort of individuality to those who know him well, and this is an important standard for judging personal identity.

There are several difficulties about this view. First, it might be argued that two people, say a father and a son, can have the same character or personality. As a claim about what has in fact ever happened this might be rejected, but it could be claimed that it need be only theoretically possible that this should occur. Then if a given disembodied spirit had the same character or personality as a recently deceased person, this would not *prove* that the spirit was the soul of the dead man.

At this point it is tempting to appeal to probability. If a disembodied spirit has the exact personality or character of a given dead man and remembers all that this man experienced, does this not put his identity with the dead man beyond reasonable doubt? The reply that would be made to this suggestion by the proponents of the sort of view we are considering would, I think, be something like this:

It makes no sense to apply the concept of probability unless we know what it would be like to have certainty. We can talk of a 10 percent probability of rain because we know what it would be like to have rain. But we cannot talk of probability where we have no idea of what it would be like to have certainty. And that is the case here: the point in question is whether there *is* any state of affairs that would constitute a disembodied spirit being the soul of a dead man. But if we have no idea of what would constitute a state of affairs, we cannot meaningfully talk about the probability of that state of affairs.

The challenge, then, is to *describe* a state of affairs that would *constitute* a disembodied person being the soul of a dead man, that would count as an instance of this in the same way many drops of water descending from the clouds count as an instance of rain. Can this challenge be answered? If so, then a disembodied spirit with the same character and memories as a dead man might make it probable that the disembodied spirit was the soul of the dead man in the same way that various pieces of evidence might make it probable that it would rain.

Note that the state of affairs that is to count as an instance need not be directly observable by us, and it may be a potential rather than an actual property of the thing. Otherwise we would have no standard for identity in the case of subatomic particles, magnetic fields, etc. But the state of affairs that is to count as an instance must, apparently, be *coherently describable* without reference to those things that are said to make it probable, just as rain is describable apart from the signs of rain.

To this modern dilemma a traditional Christian belief provides the answer. On the Christian view (as opposed to Neoplatonic misinterpretations of this view), a soul alone is not a whole person. A person consists of a soul *and* a body, and traditional Christianity offers the hope of bodily resurrection. Thus, a disembodied soul is only part of a person, and disembodied soul A can be distinguished from disembodied soul B by the fact that disembodied soul A has animated and will again animate body A and disembodied soul B has animated and will again animate body B. True, in the disembodied state this is a potentiality rather than an actuality, but any attempt to rule out potentialities as grounds for distinguishing entities would be as troublesome in microphysics as it would be in religion.

It might be argued that in theory two souls might at different times animate the same body. But on the Christian view this is a logical impossibility, not just a physical possibility. A given soul has certain capacities, which include knowing, willing, etc., but also animating a given body. The possibility that two souls might have the capacity to animate the same body can be ruled out on the same grounds that we rule out two independent omnipotent beings. For, if "omnipotent" being A and "omnipotent" being B desire different things, they cannot both have their way. Thus, at best, only one of them is omnipotent. Similarly, if soul A and soul B are both "the" soul of body C, they could will different things and the body could not do both. Thus at most, one of them is *the* soul of that body. For just as it seems reasonable to call a being omnipotent if and only if whenever it wills X to occur, X occurs, provided that X is logically possible, so it seems reasonable to call A *the* soul of body B, if and only if whenever A wills X to be done by B, B does X, provided that X is within the capacities of B.

This provides an answer to our problem, for it supplies an independent specification of a state of affairs that would count as a disembodied soul being the soul of a dead man.

It is the soul of that man if and only if it at one time animated the body of that man and will at some future time animate that body again. Of course, the body it animates again will not necessarily contain the same particles of matter as the body that soul animated at the time of death, but my body now does not contain the same particles of matter it contained ten years ago. And if a soul has the power to organize matter in such a way that new particles of matter can become part of that body over a period of time, there seems no reason to deny that it could conceivably do this instantaneously.

Does this lead to circularity? Is body B_2 the same body as B_1 only because it is animated by the same soul? On the traditional view, this is not the case. The resurrection body will be recognizably the same as the predeath body in appearance, mannerisms, etc. According to the Christian story, this was the case with the resurrected body of Christ, and according to Christian belief it is Christ's Resurrection that sets the pattern for all others. Thus, the identity of the resurrected body with the predeath body will not merely be a matter of being animated by the same soul.

Of course, our usual standard of bodily identity, namely, continuity, will not be satisfied. But we can easily imagine technological developments that would cause us to abandon this standard in everyday life, for example, the "transporter" depicted in the television series *Star Trek*. If Captain Kirk steps into the transporter at one place and disappears, and a body identical with his, with the same memories and character, appears at another place, there seems no good reason to deny that it is Captain Kirk who has appeared, even though the standard of bodily continuity has been violated. At any rate, the many thousands of people who enjoyed this program seemed to have no difficulty in accepting this situation.

We might be tempted to say that distance in time is no barrier to identifying a resurrected body as the same as a body that had died and therefore in identifying a person with that body and the appropriate memories and character as the same person as the man who died. But the discontinuity, the long period of time during which there is nothing in the universe that can be identified with the individual in question, is troubling. The Christian picture, in which the disembodied soul bridges the gap between the predeath body and the resurrected body, avoids this difficulty.

Let us recall the reason for this discussion. It was argued that belief in God's love was meaningless since no conceivable experience could disprove it. But, it was replied, experience after death could disprove God's love. The meaningfulness of experience after death was then challenged, and the discussion just concluded would seem to take care of this challenge.

Now, nothing that we have said so far gives any positive reason for believing in God or in an afterlife. All we have shown is that we must come to grips with these questions. We cannot dismiss them as meaningless. And this, after all, is what we would reasonably expect of questions that have been discussed so long and that have engaged the attention of so many first-rate minds.

2

The Accusation of Wishful Thinking

A possible reply to the statement in the last chapter that scientific discoveries do not disprove religious doctrines might go as follows: "There is one science whose findings are diametrically opposed to religion. That science is Freudian psychology, which has shown us that the ideas of God and of an afterlife are merely projections of our desires and fears." It is this accusation we will consider in this chapter.

We begin by making a few points of a mainly logical nature that will enable us to deal with some popular versions of this argument. We will then tackle the alleged scientific argument.

The first point to make is that merely offering an alternative explanation does not disprove any theory or idea. There are, for example, literally dozens of alternative theories about just how and why and by whom President Kennedy was assassinated. Besides *offering* such an alternative theory, it must be shown to be coherent and be shown to fit the known facts. Once this has been done, we are faced with two *possible* explanations. We can reasonably reject the established theory in favor of a new theory only if the new theory can be shown to be *superior* on some grounds to the established theory. As applied to a theory of "projection", which claims to account for our ideas of God and an afterlife, this means that the projection theory must first establish its credentials as a possible explanation and, second, establish its superiority to the theory that the belief in God and in a future life is rationally grounded.

The second logical point is that in general the question of the origin of our beliefs is logically irrelevant to the truth or falsity of those beliefs. If, for example, Mark Lane comes up with a plausible theory about the Kennedy assassination, the theory must be proved or disproved on its own merits. Attempted psychoanalysis of Mr. Lane, or of the supporters of the Warren Commission report, neither proves nor disproves the proposed theory. The appeal to the alleged origins of our beliefs as a substitute for arguments pro or con about the beliefs themselves is called by logicians the *genetic fallacy* and is condemned in most elementary logic books. It is a lazy man's argument. "Don't listen to him; he's a nut" has greeted a number of pioneers in ideas and has served as an excuse for not examining novel claims or uncomfortable ideas.

The final logical point is that plausible explanations of ideas in terms of their psychological origins can almost always be given on both sides of an argument and tend to cancel each other out.

The force of these last two arguments is that even if Freudian psychology were able to give a completely plausible explanation of our religious beliefs in psychological terms, this would not settle the question of the truth or falsity of those beliefs. Unless we begin with a prejudgment that a belief is false and a predisposition to accept any other possible explanation, psychological explanations of our beliefs carry little weight. The Jews of Germany in the 1930s, for example, feared persecution. It might well have been possible to explain this fear in terms of projected insecurities, etc. But unfortunately, the concentration camps were real. So unless we have already prejudged the issue of the truth of religious beliefs, we are not likely to turn to psychological explanations of such beliefs.

So far we have assumed that the psychological explanation is completely satisfactory. But if we consider the popular version of these explanations, we find immediate difficulties. One popular view, for example, is that belief in God and an afterlife is merely "wishful thinking". We believe in these things because we find it consoling or flattering to do so. This might be plausible if religion gave us a uniformly flattering or consoling picture of ourselves and our situation. But consider the view that traditional Christianity in fact gives us. Man in relation to God is not only infinitely feeble and dependent but is also condemned by his own sinfulness. God's infinite power and his perfect justice leave us in no very flattering position. True, there is also infinite mercy, but to be an object of mercy is hardly comforting to the ego. Furthermore, if our idea of the afterlife is the traditional one, it not only presents us with a real chance of terrible and eternal failure, but it also makes us responsible for even the seemingly most trivial of our actions. Now if there is one thing we all hate, it is responsibility. A good deal of our lives is spent in trying to evade one sort of responsibility or another. We can be bribed or flattered into accepting responsibility by being given power or admiration; but complete responsibility for our actions to a power infinitely superior to ourselves, without compensating power or admiration, is completely repugnant to us. If there is anyone reading who does not believe that this is true of himself, he may be superhuman, but he is much more likely to be extraordinarily good at self-deception.

The secular view of mankind, on the other hand, leaves man himself as the highest known being, the pinnacle of the universe. He is responsible only to himself, which is to say that he is not responsible. I know that the existentialists, for example, talk about man's "responsibility"; but by excluding any higher authority to which to be responsible or any real standards by which responsibility is to be judged, they effectively make the idea of responsibility an empty one. Some humanists feel a sense of responsibility to or for mankind as a whole and thus give some real content to the idea of responsibility. But "mankind as a whole" cannot call us to account or judge us; being responsible to mankind seems to mean no more than trying to live up to our own ideas of what is good for mankind, of which we are the only real judge. Of course, we can really be responsible to individuals or to groups small enough to take account of our actions. But all such responsibilities are limited, and most can be opted out of.

Traditional Christianity has compensating advantages. A meaningless life, ending in annihilation, has its own terrors, and Christianity offers us both meaning and hope of survival. But two things should be noted. First, if Christianity is to be discounted as wishful thinking because it removes fear of meaninglessness and of annihilation, then secularism should be open to the same charge, since it removes the hated ideas of an absolute superior and of real responsibility. Second, if Christianity is a mere consoling dream, one would expect it to be more uniformly consoling. It should threaten no punishments, impose no burdens. True, some modern watered-down versions of Christianity have just this quality. But I am not defending them.

So much for the easy popular explanation of Christianity as mere consolatory dreaming. We must now face the difficulty at a somewhat deeper level. The new attack might go this way: "We project our fears and repressions as well as our desires. The elements in traditional Christianity that you point to can be explained in this way."

The first comment is that this seems to be an exercise in having it both ways. All the pleasant elements in Christianity are explained away as wish fulfillment, all the unpleasant ones as fear fulfillment. Obviously we could explain away any view that has pleasant and unpleasant aspects in this way. The method is just as applicable to secularism as to Christianity. But if it applies equally to any view, it favors no one view over another.

Also, we face a difficulty here. Is Freudian psychology to be exempt from this sort of criticism or not? If it is not, then Freud's own theories can be discounted as easily as any other theory as a projection of our hopes and fears. It is thus self-refuting, like the positivists' theory. But if it claims exemption, on what grounds does it claim exemption, and how are we to be sure that other theories, even metaphysical or religious ones, cannot claim the same exemption?

As C. S. Lewis says in *Pilgrim's Regress*,[1] "Ask them if any reasoning is valid or not. If they say no then their own doctrines, being reached by reasoning, fall to the ground. If they say yes, then they will have to examine your arguments and refute them on their merits; for if some reasoning is valid, for all they know your bit of reasoning may be one of the valid bits." In reply to this we get, I think, the final reply on behalf of this sort of theory. It is the claim that the conclusions of Freudian psychology are scientifically established and that they enable us to see in detail how certain inadequacies in ourselves lead to religious beliefs. We long, for example, for a return to the childhood state

[1] *Pilgrim's Regress* (Grand Rapids, Mich.: Eerdmans, 1982), p. 62.

where a parent demanded certain behavior and rewarded and punished us, giving us a sense of "belonging" and security.

Let us make our reply in stages. First, the claim to "scientific" status for the Freudian theory may simply be a return to the confusions we discussed in the last chapter. Next, in any science, we must distinguish those elements that are properly part of the scientific theory and those philosophical ideas that may be added to these. For example, we might mention Newton's ideas of absolute space and time, which appear interspersed with the principles and calculations in his *Principia*. Now, such philosophical "extras" can be distinguished from the "working" part of the theory in that they can be removed without really affecting the rest of the theory. Scientists who held quite different views of space and time from Newton's, or no views at all, could agree with Newton's treatment of planetary motion, etc. Now, arguably the views about religion held by Freud and some of his disciples occupy this position. They are not a "working" part of Freudian psychology, and someone with quite different views on these matters, or no views at all, could agree with Freud on treating mental illness. Some of Freud's rivals—for example, Jung—were a good deal more sympathetic to religion and equally successful in treating patients. (This is not to set up Jung as an opposing authority but to point out that neither Freud nor Jung has any special authority in this area.)

As for specific theories of the mechanism behind specific religious beliefs, they often have a suspiciously ad hoc flavor. One suspects that if the beliefs were different, the theory could easily "explain" the differences. While it is unrealistic to expect the sciences of man at present to meet the scientific standards of the physical or even of the biological sciences, a theory that can be twisted with equal facility to "explain" any state of affairs really explains none.

Again, some of the specific mechanisms described by Freudians seem equally apt as an explanation for a lack of religious belief. If the Oedipus complex is as basic as Freud thought it to be, any rejection of God can surely be explained on good Freudian grounds as the desire to reject and abolish the father and have undisputed possession of "mother" earth. ("Man", say the secularists, "has come of age.")

I anticipate two sorts of reply from the defenders of the view that we have been discussing. The first would be an attempt to explain my opposition to this view on psychological grounds. A short meditation on the quote from Lewis earlier in this chapter should dispose of this not uncommon ploy.

The second defense would be a charge of superficiality or lack of expertise against my treatment. And of course, if the questions we have been discussing are psychological ones, the qualified psychologist is the expert whose opinions must be respected. If, however, they are philosophical questions, as I have suggested, then the philosopher is the expert and they the amateurs. Now the question is which sort of questions they are. And if either side can claim expertise here, it is philosophers, not psychologists, who have occasion to consider questions about the boundaries of science, the logical status of various theories, and similar matters. But we can waive any such claim of expertise here and simply ask that the arguments be considered.

3

The Accusation of Credulity

If you were to ask the average non-Christian why he found it difficult to believe in Christianity, one very frequent response would be something like this:

> Christians believe in fairy stories. They think that a child was born without a father, that a man rose from the dead, that all kinds of unheard-of events occurred. This represents a prescientific, "magical" view of the universe. But science has learned that there are scientific laws that make such things impossible. Furthermore, there is no historical basis for believing in these events. And experience shows that miracles just don't happen.

This is the kind of accusation we will examine in this chapter, both in the popular form that is summarized above and in more sophisticated forms.

Let us begin with the accusation that Christianity represents a prescientific, "magical" view of the world. Of course, Christianity is prescientific in the sense that it began before modern science began. So, for that matter, did mathematics, logic, history, and a great many other things. But that Christianity is *opposed* to a genuinely scientific view of the universe we will deny. As for the accusation that

Christianity represents a "magical" view of the universe, "magical" here either just means unscientific or antiscientific, or else it has some connection with historical beliefs in magic. This is a confusion. Magic, as believed in for many centuries, was an attempt to exert power over nature by means of words, ceremonies, mixtures of materials, etc. It was essentially an attempt of a sort of technology, an attempt to master forces that would give men power, wealth, and secret knowledge. Insofar as it was an attempt to satisfy curiosity and give power over nature, it was the ancestor of science rather than of religion.

Christianity, on the other hand, believes that certain wonderful events have occurred, sometimes as an answer to prayer. But these events were the result of the will of the Person who created nature and its laws, and could not be predicted, demanded, or forced. The effects of these events may sometimes be beneficial to men, but their purpose is to reveal something about God or to authenticate such a revelation. The whole attitude and atmosphere of magic and of Christianity are opposed. On the one hand you have the magician, with his secret knowledge, forcing certain things to occur by his spells or potions. On the other hand you have the Christian saint with his message for all men, praying that God's will be done and sometimes finding a marvelous response to his prayer. The two things are poles apart.

But this is merely preliminary skirmishing. The real point of this accusation is that the miraculous events believed in by Christians are (1) unscientific, (2) unhistorical, and (3) contrary to experience. We will consider these accusations in order.

Consider first the accusation that the Christian view of the world is unscientific or even antiscientific. This may, of course, just be the positivist objection we considered in the first chapter. But if it is not, let us see what else it may be. We will begin by briefly sketching four views of the world and what they have to say about science.

I. The Christian (or Theistic) View. On this view, the universe is the creation of a Person, whose Mind has some resemblance to our own minds (because we are made "in his image and likeness"). The universe, therefore, is intelligible; it is like a lesson set for us to master. When we discover the laws of nature, we are discovering patterns that are objectively *in* the universe, put there by God. But since God has established these patterns, he has the power to suspend them; and these suspensions are what we call miracles.

The Christian view, then, gives us a general confidence in the possibility of scientific discovery and the possibility of reaching a real understanding of the universe but leaves open the possibility of a miracle. On this view, our understanding of the universe is like our understanding of a book by an author whose intelligence we respect; the book may give us surprises, but we expect it to "make sense". It is only fair to note that this is the view of the world under which science originated and under which it developed. Scientists began looking for natural laws because they believed in a Lawgiver, and their initial success in finding laws confirmed them in this belief.

II. The Chance View. On this view, the universe is the result of random changes in some underlying material. The basic stuff of the universe is simply and inexplicably "there", and there is no reason for any of the combinations, dissolutions, and recombinations that bring into existence suns, planets, mountains, men. On this view, scientific laws are merely patterns we impose on the universe, and no event is more to be expected than any other. On this view, sudden violations of established patterns are no more unexpected, and no more meaningful, than any other event. Our "understanding" of the universe is illusory. It is like reading a book produced by monkeys pounding on a typewriter; even if we can make some sort of sense of what we have read so far, we have no reason to suppose that the next page will not be meaningless gibberish. It is hard to see how this view could be held by any scientist or how science could develop if such a view were widely held. (A view rather like this seems to be held by some existentialists.)

III. The Deterministic View. On this view, the universe is the result of the inexorable working out of laws somehow inherent in its very nature. The laws are objective, and in discovering them we are discovering something that is really there, but they are not the result of a mind. Rather, minds, our own and any others that may exist, are the results of the working out of these laws. That minds will appear at a certain stage of the development of the universe is a consequence of the laws. Indeed, everything that happens is the result of the working out of these laws. Strange and seemingly inexplicable events may sometimes occur, but they cannot be *suspensions* of the laws, for the laws cannot be suspended. They *are* explicable and can eventually be explained as the workings of laws we have not yet discovered. On this view, understanding the universe is like learning the structure of an organism that has grown in accordance with a pattern that is in its own nature and has no external cause. (Those who hold this view are often attracted to cyclical theories of the universe because they seemingly avoid questions about beginnings and ends.)

IV. The Mixed View. On this view, the universe is again the result of the inexorable working out of laws somehow inherent in its nature, but now these laws are statistical laws; they allow some scope for random variation. No more than on the deterministic view is there any conscious plan or purpose for the universe. Minds are a result, not a cause, of the universal process. But there is some "play", some variation, in the working out of the pattern; the *possibility* of minds is a consequence of the laws, but *when* minds appear, or perhaps whether or not they appear at all, depends on random factors. When strange and seemingly inexplicable events occur, they may be rare chance variations, like those rare "perfect" hands at cards.

The random variations might, however, accumulate in such a way as to cause a radical change in the course of the universe, unlikely as this may be. On this view, understanding the universe is like watching a heavy cart rolling down a rocky, bumpy hill. It is almost certain to reach the bottom, but the exact path it takes will be decided by random collisions with bumps and rocks. Still, it is just barely possible that the cart will hit a bump in such a way as to overturn and come to a halt and never reach the bottom at all. On any mixed view (of which there are many variations), the exact relation of the laws to the random variation is a very tricky point. A mixed view can in practice approach a chance view unless the laws are said to rule out absolutely some eventualities.

A point worth noting about both the deterministic view and the mixed view is that their supporters are constantly slipping into the language of the theistic view or the chance view. They often talk as if a universe allegedly without plan or purpose can "try out" or even "plan" or "force" sequences of events. They may claim to be using such language metaphorically or out of habit, but the claim is not always plausible. Similarly, even supporters of the deterministic view sometimes use language only appropriate to a chance view and talk of events "just happening" to fall out one way rather than another. Perhaps the deterministic view and the mixed view are not in the final analysis coherent views—there may be nothing at their basis but a confused mixture of elements of the theistic view and the chance view.

Sometimes supporters of a deterministic or a mixed view challenge the theistic view on the grounds that the apparent order and understandability of the universe do not imply a *personal* mind in the universe. Why not, they say, a *non*-personal mind or reason, a something rather than a someone? But the notion of a nonpersonal mind would seem to be incoherent. Anything with awareness and choice would be a person, and anything without awareness or choice could not be called a mind, nor would such a supposed "nonpersonal mind" offer any explanatory advantage over the idea of forces with inherent laws or patterns. (Of course, someone who prefers to talk about a "divine reason" rather than a "personal God" is usually merely trying to reject anthropomorphic ideas of God.)

Both the deterministic view and the mixed view have often been held by scientists, and one or the other of them is often *called* the "scientific" view of the universe. When the Christian view is called "unscientific", I think what is often meant is that it contradicts the deterministic view or the mixed view. But the first thing to notice about these four views is that three of them, the Christian view, the deterministic view, and the mixed view, seem to permit and perhaps to favor the development of science. All three views have been held by scientists in the past, and all three views are held by scientists now. Despite the claims of supporters of the deterministic view and the mixed view, they are, on the face of it, no more "scientific" than the Christian view. The second thing to notice about these views is that any choice between them cannot be a scientific choice. There is no crucial experiment that will decide between them. No amount of observation or experiment will decide among their claims. They are theories *about* science, not scientific theories. They are, in fact, philosophical theories, and any choice between them must be on the basis of philosophical arguments.

When we consider the four views on this level, we find that there is an unsurmountable objection to the second, third, and fourth views. On all of these views, our own thought processes are the result of nonrational causes that are completely beyond our control. On the chance view, these causes are random combinations and recombinations of the basic stuff of the universe. On the deterministic view, the causes are the workings of laws that existed and were at work long before any minds existed. On the mixed view, our minds are the result of a combination of law and chance. But if our thinking is caused by nonrational forces of any kind, there is no reason to suppose that our thinking is valid. It might *happen* to be valid, but we would have no way of knowing that it was. As C. S. Lewis points out,

> It is clear that everything we know, beyond our own immediate sensations is inferred from those sensations. . . . All possible knowledge, then, depends on the validity of reasoning. If the feeling of certainty which we express by words like *must be* and *therefore* and *since* is a real perception of how things stand outside our own minds really "must" be, well and good. But if this certainty is merely a feeling *in* our own minds and not a genuine insight into realities beyond them—if it merely represents the way our minds happen to

work—then we can have no knowledge. Unless human reasoning is valid no science can be true.[1]

The point about the chance view, the deterministic view, and the mixed view is not that they make it *impossible* for our reasoning to be valid, to be a true insight into realities beyond our minds. But they give us no reason at all to suppose that our reasoning *is* valid. Only conscious minds can have plans or purposes, so there is no plan or purpose that will ensure that our reasoning will attain truth. Forces that are without mind *might* happen to give us powers of valid reasoning, but they equally *might* happen to give us defective or invalid reasoning powers. And there is no reason to suppose that they would give us powers of valid reasoning rather than defective powers. Thus the views we have been considering are self-defeating in the sense that even if they were true, we could never have any good reason to think that they were true.[2]

If I pose a mathematical problem and throw some dice, the dice may *happen* to fall into a pattern that gives the answer to my problem. But there is no reason to suppose that they will. Now, on the chance view, all our thoughts are the result of processes as random as a throw of dice. On the determinist view, all our thoughts result from processes that have as little relation to our minds as the growth of a tree. On the mixed view, our minds are the result of a combination of chance and nonnatural forces.

Thus the result of these theories is to destroy our confidence in the validity of *any* reasoning—including the reasoning that may have led us to adopt these theories! Thus

---

[1] *Miracles* (San Francisco: Harper, 2001), pp. 20–22.

[2] For a very good development of this line of argument, see J. R. Lucas, *The Freedom of the Will* (Oxford: Clarendon Press, 1970), pp. 114–16.

they are self-destructive, rather like the man who saws off the branch he is sitting on. The only cold comfort they hold out is that some of our thought might happen to agree with reality.

This may be granted by "scientific" critics of Christianity so far as the chance view is concerned. But they may attempt to defend the deterministic or the mixed view. Their usual argument is that our thoughts are true reflections of the laws of the universe because they are results of these laws. The laws so work as to produce minds and to produce understanding of the laws in those minds. There are some minor difficulties about this, for example, the difficulty as to why the laws should produce false ideas of themselves in so many minds at so many times. But the major difficulty is the whole difficulty about mindless forces producing minds or understanding. Even if we see no impossibility in this, even if we grant that it *could* happen, what reason could we have for thinking that it *has* happened? Mindless forces can have no plan or purpose, by definition. To say that they necessarily produce such things is just to say that they produce them, since on the deterministic view, everything produced is produced necessarily.

It is sometimes argued that on a mixed view, minds capable of grasping truth might evolve by a process of natural selection. But natural selection works by a process whereby random variations that favor survival in a given situation enable the survivor to pass on the favorable characteristic to descendants. Even if this accounted for some practical cunning in the human species, it would be hard to show that the ability to reason theoretically has any direct survival value, especially at an early stage in the history of the human species. Again, natural selection selects out not factors that are beneficial in some general fashion but factors that are useful in surviving in a given situation, and those factors may be harmful if the situation changes. In many situations where human survival was precarious and threatened, a capacity for accepting comforting falsehoods about the universe might be more prosurvival than a capacity to search out the truth. It is only by confusedly thinking of "nature" or "the universe" as if it had conscious plans or purposes that we can make plausible an evolutionary account of man's ability to "know the nature of things".

Consider the problem in this way. Mindless forces may produce an understanding of the nature of the universe in us, or they may produce a *mis*understanding of the nature of the universe in us, just as a computer programmer may program a computer to solve problems correctly or to solve them incorrectly. Since the programmer has a mind, we presume that he would have reasons to program the computer correctly. But mindless forces cannot have reasons. If we are "programmed" by the nature of the universe, we have no more reason to suppose that we are programmed correctly than to suppose that we are programmed incorrectly. Thus, no matter how we try to evade the conclusion, the deterministic view and the mixed view are bound to destroy our confidence in the validity of our reasoning. But if no reasoning is valid, there cannot be valid reasons for accepting the deterministic view or the mixed view, or any other view. Thus, every view except the Christian view destroys our confidence in reason, and therefore in science. Therefore the Christian view is the only view that is *not* antiscientific.

Of course, we have not considered all possible views. If anyone, however, wishes to put forward a view other than those examined, he would have to specify that view and show how it offers explanatory advantages of the three views considered and how the new view avoids the disadvantages of the others. But only a view that, like the Christian view, attributes our reasoning powers to a Mind that is the cause and not the result of nature can escape the objections we made to the other views. A pantheistic conception of an "immanent" God, a "World-Soul", is open to the same objections that were fatal to the other views. For such an immanent God would be the result of irrational forces just as much as human minds are on the deterministic view. We might try to imagine a God *independent* of nature, neither the cause of nature nor caused by nature. But how could such a God serve any explanatory purpose? If nature is supposed to be totally independent of such a God, how does this guarantee the validity of *our* thinking? And if our thinking is not valid, how could we know of the existence of such a God? There really seems no alternative to some solution along the lines of the Christian view: either we admit a God who is the Lord of nature, or nature is our lord. And if nature is our lord, we could never know this—or anything else—to be true.

The objection that Christianity is unhistorical can be dealt with more briefly, for it really depends on the previous objection. If miracles are impossible, then any historical account that tells of the occurrence of miracles, as the New Testament plainly does, must be rejected as unhistorical. If miracles are tremendously improbable, then we must reject any account of them unless we get evidence of a kind that, in the nature of the case, history almost never gives us. But if the conclusions we have just reached in our discussion of the "unscientific" objections are correct, then only a view in which God is the Lord of nature can guarantee the truth of any reasoning, including historical reasoning. And if God is the Lord of nature, then miracles are not impossible, and unless we have some argument to show that they are improbable, then we cannot assume that they are. This undercuts most of the "historical" objections to miracles, for if we have no metaphysical objections to miracles, then we will have to examine the historical evidence for miracles on its merits. And if we do this we may find, as many reasonable and hardheaded men have found, that miracles are the best explanation for certain recorded events.

There may, of course, be historical objections to certain accounts of miracles—for example, one account may seem to be a mere imitation of another, or other historical evidence may render that particular supposed miracle improbable, and so on. But the general objection to miracles is not based on anything peculiar to history as such but on philosophical grounds.

The final objection to miracles is the supposed objection from experience. Most versions of this objection trace back more or less indirectly to a famous objection by David Hume, which goes as follows:

A miracle is a violation of the laws of nature; and as a firm and unalterable experience has established these laws, the proof against a miracle, from the very nature of the fact, is as entire as any argument from experience can possibly be imagined. . . . Nothing is esteemed a miracle, if it ever happens in the common course of nature. It is no miracle that a man, seemingly in good health, should die on a sudden; because such a kind of death, though more unusual than any other, has yet been frequently observed to happen. But it is a miracle that a dead man should come to life; because that has never been observed in any age or country. There must, therefore, be a uniform experience against every miraculous event, otherwise the event would not merit the appellation. And as a uniform experience amounts to a proof, there is here a direct and full proof, from the nature of the fact, against the existence of any miracle; nor can such a proof be destroyed, or the miracle rendered credible, but by an opposite proof, which is superior.[3]

Obviously, we must interpret Hume's objection in such a way that it is not an objection to any unique event. After all, up to a certain date, there was "uniform experience" against a man setting foot on the moon. It must, therefore, be a certain *class* or *kind* of events we are eliminating. But what class? Miracles? But this begs the whole question. As an "argument" against the allegation that miracles occur, we have the assertion that there is uniform experience against miracles—in other words, the unsupported assertion that miracles do not happen!

The only respectable way of interpreting what Hume says here, I think, is to take him as arguing that past experience gives us some kind of assurance that laws of nature *cannot* be suspended. (If it merely alleges that they have *never* been suspended, it is just "miracles don't happen" in a new guise.) We interpret Hume, then, as saying that experience proves that natural laws are "unsuspendable". But how *could* experience show any such thing? Any such theory must be a philosophical interpretation of experience, not the direct result of experience. And if we ask *what* philosophical theory it is, it looks suspiciously like our old friend the deterministic view, which as we saw has a fatal defect.

So we conclude that the "unhistorical" and "contrary to experience" objections depend essentially on the "unscientific" accusation and that far from being antiscientific, the Christian view is the only one that gives us any reason to trust any kind of reasoning, including scientific reasoning. Thus it would seem that the whole line of objections sketched at the beginning of this chapter fails.

[3] *Enquiries*, ed. L. A. Selby-Bigge (Oxford University Press, 1955), pp. 114f.

4

The Accusation of Immorality

Perhaps the most frequent cause of the loss of religious belief or the failure to accept religious belief is the "problem of evil". Seeing the cruelty and corruption, the pain and suffering, the apparent senseless waste in the world, many honest and decent men have been repelled. "If God existed," they say, "he would not permit all this. And if some all-powerful Being sees and permits all this, he is a demon, not a God worthy of worship." But strangely enough, Christians are just as familiar with evil as those who speak in this way, and they draw very different conclusions from what they observe. Neither side knows any facts that the other is ignorant of; it is a question of how these facts are evaluated. And the facts in question are not mere descriptions of phenomena— they are evaluations of the phenomena. Specifically, they are moral evaluations; certain things are seen not merely as inconvenient or disagreeable but rather as morally evil. And those who acquiesce in these evils are seen as immoral, if they are not merely deluded; as knaves, unless they are fools.

Since we have here an essentially moral problem, let us consider the main theories about morality and their bearings on this problem. For our purposes we can simplify these theories down to three main alternatives:

I. The Relativist Theory. On this theory, moral judgments are *completely* relative to the individual. This does not only mean that it may be wrong for you, but not for me, to sell my car, spank my children, or make love to my wife; that would be common ground for many moral theories. Complete relativism means that moral judgments are no more than individual opinions, with no validity for anyone but oneself. This theory grants that groups or tribes or nations may share opinions and may attempt to enforce them by laws, by group pressures, and so on. But it denies any objective validity to these opinions. Murder is wrong for me if I think it is, right for you if you think it is. On one interpretation of them, Hamlet's words express this theory exactly: "There is nothing either good or bad, but thinking makes it so." Some exponents of this theory seem to feel that a man *can* do evil, by violating his *own* standards. But the majority of the supporters of this theory seem to feel that no one does wrong in his own eyes. When we do a thing we believe it to be right, otherwise we would not do it. On either interpretation this theory renders moral indignation impossible; for on the one interpretation, no one (not Hitler, not Stalin, not Judas) ever does anything wrong, and on the other interpretation, anyone who has done wrong has done so by violating *his* moral code, which may be very different from yours. Thus we can never condemn anyone else as evil.

But of course, if we can condemn no one, we cannot condemn God. The relativistic view is incompatible with any *moral* objection to the universe, or to anything else for that matter. Thus the man who feels moral indignation at the evil in the world and rejects Christianity on that account either is not a relativist or is a very inconsistent one. Of course, the relativist may claim to be merely pointing out inconsistencies in the Christian position, but we then move to another realm of discourse; the objection becomes a logical one, not a moral one. It is an accusation of illogicality, not of immorality.

II. The Theistic View. On this view, morality somehow has its origin in God. On one simple but not very satisfactory version of this view, what is right is simply what God commands, whatever that may be. God has enjoined love and forbidden hatred, but he might just as well have commanded hatred and forbidden love. No problem of evil can arise on this view, since whatever God wills to happen is good, and thus all the apparent evils about us are good, since nothing happens without God's will.

This view has been held by some Christians, but it is not the Christian view. On the Christian view, morality depends on the nature of God and on the nature of the things he has made. It is part of the Christian message that God is love, and a Being who commanded hatred and forbade love could not be God. If it is a moral truth, grounded in the nature of a God who is love, that to allow or inflict useless suffering on innocent people is always wrong, and if it is a physical fact that slowly burning the body of a person causes suffering, then allowing or causing an innocent person to be slowly burned for no good reason would always be wrong. This could be changed by changing physical facts (for example, God could make slow burning delightful or beneficial). If the moral truths are changeable (for example, if they rest on a commanded duty, such as circumcision, which could be made not a duty by a changed command), then the consequential wrongness could be changed. But unless one or the other were changed, the wrongness could not be taken away.

Now, on this view, there can be a problem of evil, since some things that happen in the world seem to be contrary to what a loving God would permit. But the problem must somehow be soluble, since the events we condemn and the moral law by which we condemn them are both traceable to the same Source. If God is what Christianity says he is, he is the God of love and justice, and also the God who permits apparently useless suffering. It must be, then, that there is a reconciliation. (Perhaps the suffering is *not* useless, for example.) Thus evil is a problem for Christianity but not an objection to it. The view that admits a problem holds out the hope of a solution.

III. The Absolute Moral Law View. On this view, there is a moral law that is objective and does not depend on individual opinions but that is also independent of God. If causing useless suffering is wrong, it would be wrong whether God existed or not. Supporters of this view often think of the moral law as impersonal and inexorable, rather as we sometimes think of nature. Disagreeing with the moral law is as useless and as silly as disagreeing with any fact of nature—entropy or atomic energy, for example. The moral law exists whether we like it or not.

On one interpretation of this view, God does not exist. The moral law itself is the Ultimate Reality or Highest Thing. What must be obeyed is an It, not a He. Obviously no problem of evil can exist on this view, for you can blame only persons, not facts. If a man goes unprotected into space, he dies. If a man disobeys the moral law, he suffers for it, and so do others. It is equally silly to blame the moral law as to blame space.

The second interpretation says that God coexists with the absolute moral law without either depending on the other in any way. One way of making sense of this is to think of the moral law as something God *transcends*. He is not limited by the moral law just as he is not (on the view of many philosophers and theologians) limited by space or time. On this view, God is "beyond good and evil". But it is hard to see how there could be any problem of evil on this view. For, if God transcends good and evil, it is as useless to judge him by moral standards as to judge him by spatial standards.

The final interpretation of the absolute moral law view says that a God exists but is *subject* to the moral law. There is a Creator of the universe, but this Creator may be imperfect in some ways. His imperfections may include moral imperfections, as measured by the standards of the absolute moral law. On this view, the existence of evil is incompatible not with the *existence* of God but with the *moral perfection* of God. We could, of course, quibble about whether a morally imperfect being would deserve the name of God. So long as we are clear about what we *mean*, we can say whichever we like. On the one meaning the question will be, "Given the evil in the world, is God good?" while on the other meaning the question will be, "Given the evil in the world, is the Creator of the universe God?"

Now that we have surveyed the main possibilities, we can see that only the fourth and seventh—the second interpretation of the theistic view and the last interpretation of the absolute moral law view—give us a *problem* of evil. If there is no real standard of good and evil, or if the standard is whatever God arbitrarily says it is, or if the Highest Reality is impersonal, or if God is "above" good and evil, there is no problem. I will discuss some of these possibilities in due course. But for the remainder of this chapter, I am going to go on the assumption that there *is* a problem of good and evil, and I will try to do what I can to solve it. In a way, it does not matter at this stage which of the two alternatives that give us a problem we prefer. In either case, we have an apparent incongruity between the moral law as we understand it, and what God does or permits.

Let us begin by clearing up some misunderstandings. What evils or apparent evils are we to consider as counting, or apparently counting, against the goodness of God?[1] Almost anyone who admits the existence of an objective moral law at all thinks that one of the principles of that moral law is that one person cannot be blamed for what another is responsible for. And a person cannot be responsible unless he has a genuinely free choice. Thus, if some evil consists of genuinely free choices by persons who are responsible for these choices, God cannot be responsible for these choices. Of course, someone may wish to hold that *no* human actions are genuinely free and that no human being is ever responsible for his choices. This is the view called *hard determinism*, and if it is true then we are merely puppets in God's hands. But if this view is true, then human beings are not moral agents, and moral evil, as usually conceived of, does not exist. No man lies, as we ordinarily conceive of lying; he merely utters whatever God makes him utter. No man is cruel, as we ordinarily conceive of cruelty; he merely acts in certain ways in which he is made to act by God. Thus, if hard determinism is true, God is the only moral agent. But, although some Christians have been hard determinists, hard determinism is not the Christian view. It is, in fact, incompatible with Christianity, for Christianity rests on human responsibility. Its basic call is to repentance; its

---

[1] On any view that, like Christianity, holds that the soul is immortal, death will not be an evil in itself, though suffering caused by death may be.

basic doctrine is the redemption of sinful mankind. If only God is a moral agent, then these doctrines are nonsensical.

Of course, Christianity is not incompatible with the idea that many persons are less responsible than they appear. Christ forbade his followers to judge others, lest they be judged. He specifically said that many of the first would be last and the last first, that whores and traitors would enter the Kingdom ahead of respectable religious teachers and officials. But unless the normal situation is that most of us are responsible for most of our actions, Christianity makes no sense at all. It promises forgiveness to sinners, and unless we are moral agents we cannot be sinners, and forgiveness is a charade.

Thus, for all moral evil, that is, for all choices made by persons other than God, the Christian response is that these persons are genuinely free moral agents, and the responsibility for their actions rests with them. Where this is not true, for example, in the case of a falsehood or a killing by an insane person, there is no *moral* evil.

However, it might be argued that God *is* morally responsible for choosing to create free moral agents who he knew would make evil choices. He might, as an alternative, have (1) created *no* free agents, or (2) created only those free agents who he foresaw would make no evil moral choices. Let us grant that God could have done the first of these. To show that he was morally blameworthy for creating free agents, it would be necessary to prove that a state of affairs with free moral agents, some or all of whom make some evil choices, is not morally preferable to a state of affairs with no free agents. I do not see how this could be proved, and I have never seen any attempt to prove it, though I have sometimes seen it assumed. It seems to me that very few would choose, either for themselves or for their children, a state of being a robot rather than a free moral agent, even a free moral agent who sometimes sinned.

The second possibility may not in fact make sense. It seems to envision a sort of precensorship, as if God could review "possible people" and not create any who would commit any sin whatever. This may be a totally inadequate notion of God's mode of choice. But, supposing that it does make sense, it seems to contain a hidden assumption. This assumption is that a world of persons who never make bad moral choices is preferable to a world in which bad moral choices are made but become means of moral and spiritual growth. Or, putting it another way, the assumption is that a good God would prefer sinless people to saints who were at some earlier time sinners. It seems to me that we have no positive evidence for this assumption at all, and the Christian who reflects on Christ's choice of apostles and on the great Saints through the ages may find some evidence in his religious beliefs for the contrary of this assumption.

In fact, I suspect that if we are to make any imaginative effort to understand God's choice of what persons to create, we would do better to imagine him creating Peter or Augustine or Thomas or Gilbert or Jack, preferring in some sense that they should never sin but loving them as persons and striving mightily to turn even their evil choices to eventual good.

I conclude, then, that the effort to make God responsible in any way for moral evil cannot succeed and that if any moral charge is to succeed as against the goodness or the existence of God, it must be the charge that he permits or even causes unnecessary "physical evil", that is, unnecessary pain or suffering.

I take it that most people would be willing to grant that there is necessary suffering, suffering that could not be eliminated without eliminating a good thing of which that suffering is a necessary condition. Let us begin with some trivial but relatively uncontroversial cases.

Consider, for example, the mountain climber or the football player. The climber could reach the top of the peak by helicopter with no pain at all. The football player could reach the goal unhurt and unthreatened by bribing all the opposing players to let him slip by them. But neither would find reaching their goal in this way worth doing. Unless they had genuinely overcome the obstacles themselves, in the face of pain and danger, they would feel no sense of accomplishment. Since these objectives *could* be obtained without pain, however, they are perhaps not a good example. A game can be defined as an activity whose end result has no intrinsic value, and life is not a game.

A better image is the efforts, pains, and frustrations necessary to master any art or science or discipline. To be able to play like Heifetz, or philosophize like Wittgenstein, is not really separable from the long years of practice and playing, or the long years of wrestling with philosophical problems. But even if the end result could be achieved without pain, it would thereby be less valuable.

But the best examples come from the area of personal relations. Anyone who has been sincerely in love has felt the impulse to do something for his beloved that costs him pain or effort. The greater the love, the greater the willingness, even the desire, to suffer and endure for the beloved. The love of a young man for his betrothed may make him happy to give up smoking to buy her an engagement ring. Beyond and above this easy sacrifice are the heights of self-sacrifice and martyrdom.

Now, the whole Christian answer to the problem of apparently useless suffering is that no suffering is really useless.

Our examples have shown us that suffering *can* be necessary to a greater good. The Christian belief is that the point of our whole existence, immeasurably more important than climbing a particular mountain, mastering a certain discipline, or marrying a certain woman, is to become a person of a certain sort. To become a person of this sort, sacrificial love, love that genuinely *costs* us something, is necessary. And pain is a necessary condition of such love. All the suffering in this world is bound up with this aim and this necessity. That is the Christian answer to the problem of pain. Christianity has no other answer. We can explore this answer in all its dimensions, we can understand it more and more deeply, but we cannot go beside it or behind it or beyond it. This is *the* Christian answer.

The immediate reply to this Christian answer to the problem of pain is to argue that it is immensely implausible as an answer to the question of why this or that particular piece of suffering was permitted. And this is quite true. Christianity does not have, and does not profess to have, an answer to each particular question as to why each particular piece of suffering was permitted. It has a general answer but not many particular answers. In many cases where the suffering is our own, we can see, or think we can see, the good results. We can sometimes see results in other cases. But if we are curious about such results in others, our only answer is likely to be, "What is that to you? Follow me!" (John 21:22).

It might also be claimed that the *general* answer is implausible or improbable. This may mean one of two things. It may mean that there is some a priori unlikelihood in the solution. But I do not know how this could be established. Or it may mean that it is implausible in case 1, in case 2, in case 3, etc., and so that finally it is implausible in the majority of cases.

Let us examine this second idea. Suppose that I claim that most Americans marry for money. You may disprove this by showing that in case 1, John and Mary married for love; in case 2, that Sam and Sally married because Sally was pregnant; that in case 3, Dick and Betty did not have a penny between them when they married; and so on. You give, in other words, an *alternative* explanation in each case. But in the case of apparently useless suffering, nothing positive is put on the other side of the question.

The situation is rather like someone who challenges the claim that most Americans marry for love by professing himself unsatisfied with that explanation in a number of cases but without having any alternative explanation. The fact that in the nature of the case, he could have very little information, and the fact that he proposed no alternative explanation, would both be against him. Yet this is very like the case of pain. I know little enough about the effects of suffering on my own character, and very little of its effects on anyone else. If I accept the Christian explanation, it is not because of an accumulation of evidence from particular cases but because a general view of the universe, of which this explanation is a part, makes sense to me. I suspect that the critic's charge of implausibility means no more than that a different theory makes sense to him. This can be debated, but it must be debated on the level of the whole theory in question.

One final point: some have seen in dualism, the theory of a good "God" and a bad "God" in eternal struggle, a solution to the problem of evil. As we saw on page 34, there cannot be two omnipotent beings, so neither "God" would be all-powerful; this removes one element of the problem of evil since the good "God" might not be *able* to prevent evil. But what would we mean by calling one "God" good and the other evil? There would have to be some more ultimate source of morality to justify this judgment, as there would have to be some more ultimate source of existence to account for the existence of the two limited "Gods". So dualism, far from solving the problems of evil, forces us back to the same problems and solutions we have discussed.

In the second part of this book, I will try to say something more positive about the Christian view of suffering and its uses. But for the moment I conclude that the Christian acceptance of suffering does not justify the charge of immorality and that the problem of evil is not fatal to the idea of God's love.

5

The "Empirical Bogey"

Even if the arguments in the last four chapters have convinced someone that Christians are not talking nonsense, not merely indulging in wishful thinking, not merely credulous when they entertain the possibility of miracles, and not immoral when they worship a God who permits evil, a final difficulty may remain. It may take something like this form:

> Christianity arose when the universe seemed a smaller and cozier affair. Now that science has shown us the true age and size of the universe, we can no longer accept the idea of a God who is personally concerned with our conduct or our consciences. If any creative power is the cause of the physical universe, it has no interest in us. The idea of God explains nothing and changes nothing. For modern man, God is dead.

Now, this is hardly worthy of the name of argument. From the knowledge that the universe is very large and old, it does not follow that God takes no interest in man unless we add further premises. And as we will see, these further premises have no plausibility at all. But the emotional force of the size and age of the universe, once it is imaginatively grasped, is very great. To many people the universe, as science shows it to us, does not *feel* like the sort of universe that would be made by a personal god. And since many people think mainly with their emotions, there seems to them to be an argument. C. S. Lewis once called this "argument" the "empirical bogey".

If we analyze the image or idea that seems to bridge the gap between the age and size of the universe and God's supposed indifference to man, I think that we find something like the following: In our own experience, the larger a thing is or the longer it lasts, the more difficult we find attending to the details or parts of that thing. The bigger a thing is, the more we have to deal with it in a general, abstract, impersonal sort of way. This is because we cannot perceive all of it at once, and when we are attending to one part, we cannot attend to other parts. By the time we get to Z, we have forgotten A. We find we cannot see the forest for the trees, and so we are forced to forget the individual trees and think of the forest in general terms.

This experience of our own makes us tend to think of God as a sort of harried executive with many problems with which to deal. Naturally, with a universe as big and old as ours, many things must be attended to, and a small, obscure planet like ours, much less any individual on it, will be lost in the shuffle.

However, not only the Christian idea of God but also any even moderately sophisticated philosophical idea of God shows how silly is this image of God as the harried chief executive of the universe. Even if God were a very great but still limited being, a closer look at our own experience should show us that a creator can grasp his work as a whole and in all its details, even when the work is as rich and complex as, for example, J. R. R. Tolkien's *Lord of the Rings*.

An executive, after all, is trying to deal with beings he has not made and whom he does not completely control. But if God is the Creator of the universe, he is much more like the author than the executive.

But, of course, both religion and philosophy give us the idea of God as a Being without any limitations at all. A dull man can attend to only one thing at a time—he cannot both drive and talk, for example. A somewhat more intelligent man can deal with more than one thing at a time, and so on. Every man has limitations, and perhaps none of us can give completely adequate attention to even two things. Similarly, one man forgets easily, another has a better memory, and so on. But if God exists at all, he has no limitations at all. As we shall see, God may transcend time altogether. But even if we find this idea too puzzling, any adequate idea of God will be an idea of a being who can simultaneously give his full attention to any number of things, who never forgets or neglects anything. Any being with less than these capabilities would not be God.

Now, it might be granted that God is *aware* of our doings and thoughts and desires, but, to put the objection crudely, why should he be *interested* in us? Aren't we pretty small fish in a very vast sea? Doesn't he, so to speak, have more important things to worry about? The assumption here is somewhat more subtle. Instead of foisting human limitations onto God, we are attributing to him a human scale of values. We think of God as perhaps interested in galaxies but not in planets, or, if he is interested in human beings at all, as being interested in Hitler or Churchill but not in the ordinary soldier or peasant.

Philosophy can take us a certain way here. It can point out that importance is not proportional to size. A six-foot man, as C. S. Lewis pointed out, is not more important than

a five-foot man. But if there were a *logical* relation between
size and importance, even a small difference in size should
make a small difference in importance. Furthermore, we
can see that the qualities we tend to think important, such
as being the political leader of a large country, may not be
the qualities God thinks important. So far philosophy can
take us.

But Christianity goes further. It makes the astonishing
claim that God cares intensely for each one of us, that he
loves us and wants our love. If this is true, then it does no
good to say that we are "not interested in God"; he is interested in us, and that is what counts. Christianity leaves no
ground at all for the comfortable idea that God doesn't care
for us and that we needn't care for him and that we can go
our separate ways like polite strangers. If Christianity is true,
then there is no question of going our separate way. Our
separate way to where? All roads lead either toward God or
away from him. We exist only because God has created us
and sustains us in existence. He has a purpose for us, a
purpose we can reject, since we are free. But to ignore the
whole question is the height of folly.

Of course, if Christianity is false, it doesn't matter how
relevant it would be if true. But if someone says, "It doesn't
matter whether God exists or not", then he either is not
understanding the Christian idea of God or else is incred-
ibly confused. (In many cases, both are true.)

What some of these people seem to mean is that even if
God existed, we would have to make our own moral decisions. In a way, of course, this is true. If we are genuinely
free, we are free to choose for or against morality or conscience. But the existence of God obviously makes a great
difference in what morality *is*. Many of the people we are
talking about hold the view we called the relativist view, in

one of its two forms. But if God exists, not all ideas of right and wrong are relative. God's ideas would occupy a privileged position, to say the least.

Another thing that might be meant by saying God's existence would change nothing might be this: if we hold what I called the absolute moral law position, then the moral law ought to be obeyed whether or not God exists, for God is either independent of or subordinate to the moral law. As we will see, there is an element of misunderstood truth in this position.

But I think that very often the idea that God's existence "wouldn't matter" rests on just the confusion we have been discussing. What is meant is that even if some Creator or Ruler of the universe did exist, he would be far too busy to bother with us. A good deal of the modern talk about the "irrelevance" of God seems to me to rest on just this basis. And we have seen how inadequate this basis is.

The objection that the idea of God explains nothing is more complex, and we will not be able to deal with it fully until our discussion of God in a later chapter. But some preliminary things can be said now. This objection often rests on a certain psuedohistorical idea of the relation between science and religion. According to this idea, man starts out by attributing all striking phenomena to a God or gods— the lightning is the spear of a god, the thunder the voice of a god, and so on. As science discovers the cause of these phenomena, man has to abandon the idea that God or gods are responsible for these phenomena. He then uses God as an explanation for other events he does not understand— the origin of species of animals, for example. But science again provides a "natural" explanation of this, and religion retreats. According to this view, God is brought in only to fill gaps in our scientific knowledge: he is "the God of the

gaps". But the few gaps that remain in our scientific knowledge, such as the origin of life, or the origin of the universe, are now being closed, leaving no place for God.

This story is, in fact, historically false (as, by the way, is
the idea that educated men at the time of Christ did not
believe that the universe was tremendously vast and ancient).
For example, phenomena like lightning and thunder were
not scientifically understood until quite recent times, but
educated believers had long abandoned primitive ideas of
thunder as God's voice, etc., by the time of Christ. But this
is relatively unimportant. More important is what believers
actually believed and the bearings of science on what they
believed. A Jew at the time of Christ believed that God
was the *ultimate* explanation of all phenomena. In some
cases—for example, human conception and birth—he knew
some of the "secondary causes", some of the means God
used to bring about a result. But he gave thanks to God for
the birth of a child even though he knew that certain actions
of his own had been part of the cause for the birth of that
child.

In other cases, he did not know the secondary causes of
an event, and he might in that case quite reasonably have
attributed these events to the direct action of God. If you
believe that all the pictures in a room were painted either
by the teacher or by one of his pupils with the help of the
teacher, it makes sense to compliment the teacher on any
pictures you think are good, and if you do not know that a
pupil painted a given picture, it is reasonable to believe that
the teacher himself painted it. The Jews also believed that
certain wonderful events, such as the deliverance from Egypt,
had occurred by the direct intervention of God, just as you
might believe that a certain picture in the room was so
good that it *must* be by the teacher.

What science can show us about this is that there are in fact certain secondary causes of which we were unaware. Thunder is not ordinarily caused by the direct action of God but by masses of air striking together, just as conception is not ordinarily caused by the direct action of God but by the coming together of a man and a woman. But science has nothing to say about the question of whether the *ultimate* cause of all these events is God or whether God sometimes does things directly that he ordinarily does by means of secondary causes. Both of these are philosophical or religious questions. Finding that more pictures than you thought were painted by the pupils does not disprove the existence of the teacher: it may be that the activity of the pupils can be explained only by the presence of a teacher. Knowing that the pupils ordinarily do something—for example, do the lettering on signs for the pictures—does not show that the teacher may not occasionally do it himself.

Some people seem to feel that a God who "wound up" the universe and left it to tick away according to unchangeable laws would be tolerable but that a God who "interferes" with the universe at any point would somehow render the universe chaotic. But if we think about our own experience with our fellow human beings, we realize that even the best set of unbreakable rules cannot handle all the situations free human beings can create. We can, of course, make individuals slaves to the rules, but can we imagine God doing this? Christ said in another context that the law was made for man, not man for the law. Even sillier than the idea of God as the harassed chief executive is the idea of God as the great bureaucrat saying, "I'd like to help you, but rules are rules."

And, of course, we can see that in our own experience a state of affairs where rules that take care of ordinary situations but can be suspended in special cases is far from chaotic. It is, in fact, far more reasonable than a state of affairs where rules are absolute.

To take two examples of the difficulty: First, God may or may not have intervened directly in some way to create life. We may never know whether he did, or science may discover some secondary causes by which God brought life into the universe. But in either case, we may have good reasons for believing that God is the ultimate Source of life.

Second, there is the question of the origin of the human soul. We know the secondary causes by which human bodies come into existence, and we believe that every human body comes "equipped" with a human soul. Thus in one sense we understand how human souls originate: the process follows laws we can understand and use for prediction. But if Christians are right in believing that the soul is a nonmaterial substance that can exist without a body (and does, between death and resurrection), then we do not understand the origin of the soul at all. We simply find a soul with each body born. It is a very old Christian belief that God directly creates the human soul before birth. The emergence of a human soul is a predictable event, following certain regular rules and patterns, but this does not mean it is not due to the direct intervention of God. In other cases, we know that secondary causes are ordinarily the immediate cause of certain events, for example, thunder; but this does not mean either that God is not the ultimate cause of these events or that in some cases God may not be the direct cause of these events.

Of course, we may deny that events have *any* ultimate explanation. But if there is no ultimate explanation, this leaves the intermediate explanations in a peculiar position.

If young Johnny asks his mother for an explanation of something and does not understand the explanation, he can ask for an explanation of the explanation. If this happens several times, his mother, in exasperation, says, "Just because" to his latest request for an explanation. But if the chain of explanation ends in a "just because", do the intermediate explanations really explain? Consider a short series of this kind: "Why did you buy that soap, Mommy?" "Because the man on television said it was the best soap." "Why did he say it was the best soap?" "It was written down for him to say." "Why was it written down for him to say?" "Just because, Johnny; go run and play." Does Johnny really have a satisfactory explanation of why his mother bought the soap? A chain of explanations ending in midair is not a great deal better than no explanation at all.

So I conclude that not only is an ultimate explanation needed, but unless one is forthcoming, all intermediate explanations are left "suspended in midair". As we have seen, chance or absolute natural law cannot be the ultimate explanation, and God seems to be the only possibility left.

Let us be clear what we have and have not accomplished in the first part of this book. We have repelled certain common attacks on Christianity, and in repelling some of these attacks, we have begun to find some positive reasons for accepting Christianity, or at least theism, as the only account of the universe that leaves room for science, for moral responsibility, for an ultimate explanation. But even if all these attacks have been successfully repelled, we need to say much more about the positive reasons for accepting Christianity. To these positive reasons we shall turn in the second part of this book.

PART II

REASONS

6

The Nature of Faith

In the first part of this book, we showed that the Christian faith is not nonsensical and that none of the common arguments against it is successful. Thus we showed that it is not unreasonable to believe in Christianity. Some Christians seem to feel that this is all reason can be expected to do in this area and that then faith must take over. That this is not the biblical view or the traditional Christian view is, I think, clear from a study of the scriptures and a study of history. It is also, I believe, based on a misunderstanding of the nature of faith. Faith must be based on reasons, and the reasons must be good ones. I shall argue in the second half of this book that there *are* good reasons for accepting the Christian faith and that we need not fall back on some "will to believe", which does not rest on any evidence.

First, however, let us consider the nature of faith itself. Faith is a special kind of belief, and the best way to understand faith is first to understand the nature of belief. The weakest sort of belief is what I will call "*mere* belief". When we are asked a question, we sometimes give an answer in a qualified way, not claiming to know or even to be sure of our answer: "What is the distance between the earth and the sun?" "Ninety-three million miles, I believe." By saying, "I believe", we emphasize that we *merely* believe—we do not *know*. We also use "I think" for this sense of belief: "I *think* it's ninety-three million miles (but I don't know for sure)." In this use of belief, we would be surprised but not dumbfounded to find we were wrong. We are not absolutely certain, and we are not giving our authority for what we say. If someone tells us afterward that he relied on our statement and it was incorrect, we reply, "I only said I *believed* (thought) it was ninety-three million miles; if it was important, you should have checked." Belief in this sense of "believe" has little to do with religious faith.

Belief in the stronger sense, where we are confident in what we believe and would be astounded if we were wrong, seems to have three major characteristics: (1) we must have some understanding of what we claim to believe; (2) we must be prepared to take action appropriate to our stated belief; and (3) we must have some reason for our belief. The first condition is obvious enough. If I claim to believe some statement and it later turns out that I do not even know what that statement means, you do not take my claim to belief very seriously. I am merely repeating a form of words, not really believing anything.

The second condition is one we constantly invoke in practice. If someone claims to believe that some kind of behavior, smoking, for example, is very undesirable and should be avoided but goes on smoking, we say, "He doesn't really believe what he says. If he did, he'd stop smoking." Of course, a person may act as if something were true without believing it (for example, because he is pretending), and a person may believe something and still not act in ways in which people who believe that thing act. But some connection between belief in the stronger sense and action seems to exist and to be acknowledged in everyday life.

The third condition, that we must have some reason for belief in the strong sense, is less obvious. The point is that if we merely have a hunch or a feeling, we may say that we believe in the weak sense: "I believe that man is dishonest." "Why?" "No reason I can put my finger on. I just have a feeling." But unless we are either unreasonable or very confident of our hunches or feelings, we do not base a claim to certainty on such grounds. Ordinarily, "*Why* do you believe that?" is a question that requires a reasonable answer, and "For no reason" is not an acceptable answer.

Religious faith plainly shares these characteristics of belief in the strong sense. We might very well challenge a claim that a child had faith in the doctrine of the Trinity on the grounds that the child was too young to understand it. The child might, of course, have faith that whatever he was taught was true, whether he could understand it or not; but this is not the same as having faith in the Trinity. We often use the connection between faith and action to judge the faith of others: the martyr, for example, is preeminently a witness to his faith because only a man who really believed would act as he acts. Finally, the idea that faith must be based on good reasons has good authority. For example, 1 Peter 3:15, "Always be prepared to make a defense to any one who calls you to account for the hope that is in you", and 2 Peter 1:16, 19, "For we did not follow cleverly devised myths when we made known to you the power and coming of our Lord Jesus Christ, but we were eyewitnesses of his majesty . . . and we have the prophetic word made more sure. You will do well to pay attention to this as to a lamp shining in a dark place, until the day dawns and the morning star rises in your hearts." Presumably the modern Christian does not have the same evidence the apostles had, but any claim that Christian belief should be without evidence or contrary to evidence is against the whole tenor of the New Testament.

How, then, is faith *different* from belief in the strong sense? The differences seem to me to lie in (1) the kind of confidence involved, (2) the degree of understanding expected, (3) the kind of action to which we are committed, and (4) the kinds of reasons we have for our belief.

The kind of confidence is different in that faith is generally regarded as more unshakable than belief and also as more personal. Faith involves trust in a person, not just confidence in the truth of a statement, as when we speak of a child's faith in his father and mother. Religious faith is of course primarily faith in God: not only belief in his existence and in what he has revealed to man but also *trust* in him. Faith is also usually regarded as on a special level of certainty: one good dictionary defines faith as "unquestioning belief". We will consider some problems that arise in connection with this idea presently.

Faith also differs from ordinary belief in that we are usually willing to grant that we only partially understand the object of our faith. God is by definition infinitely greater than we are and thus only partly comprehensible to us. His revelation to us is full of things we do not fully understand: the Christian community is always growing in knowledge and appreciation of its rich heritage. Of course, if we understood *nothing* of what we believe, our belief would be empty; but *partial* understanding is what we should expect in the nature of the case.

The third distinctive feature of faith is the nature of our commitment to it. We may strongly believe certain statements without being willing to suffer or die for them. But when a man suffers or dies for an idea or ideal, be it God, reason, democracy, Communism, or whatever it may be, we speak of his faith in God, in reason, in democracy, in Communism. A man who has nothing for which he will die or suffer may have opinions or beliefs, but he has no faith in anything. In due course we will consider the objection that it is a good thing to lack faith in anything, to have *only* beliefs and opinions for which we would not die or suffer greatly. But that faith has this characteristic most people would agree.

Finally, faith is distinguished from both belief and knowledge by the sort of reasons we have for it. If we know something by experience or have a conclusive deductive argument for it, we say that we *know*, not that we have belief *or* faith. Thus, evidence of a certain degree of strength rules out faith. But if we *merely* have a probability, a gambler's chance of being right, we do not speak of having faith either. Still, it is not just a matter of a degree of confidence exactly in between knowledge and probability. A man who has faith does not say, "I know", but neither does he say, "I am 99 percent certain", any more than he says, "I am 80 percent certain."

On the whole I think the best formula is that given by C. S. Lewis: "assent to a proposition which we think so overwhelmingly probable that there is a psychological exclusion of doubt although not a logical exclusion of dispute".[1] It is this kind of confidence that we generally have in our fundamental beliefs, whatever these may be. A convinced materialist may not say it is logically impossible to disprove the possibility of a miracle, but if he is faced with the report of one, then, as Lewis says:

> He knows that he cannot, there and then, produce a refutation of the miracle which would have the certainty of mathematical demonstration; but the formal possibility that

[1] "On Obstinacy in Belief", in *The World's Last Night, and Other Essays* (Harvest Books / Harcourt, 2001), p. 16.

the miracle might after all have occurred does not really trouble him any more than a fear that water might not be H and O. Similarly the Christian does not necessarily claim to have demonstrative proof; but the formal possibility that God might not exist is not necessarily present in the form of the least actual doubt. Of course there are Christians who hold that such demonstrative proof exists, just as there may be materialists who hold that there is demonstrative disproof. But then whichever of them is right (if either is) while he retained the proof or disproof would not be believing or disbelieving but knowing. We are speaking of belief or disbelief in the strongest degree, but not of knowledge.[2]

Lewis follows this passage with the definition we have just given.

Now, anyone who holds a faith or belief of this kind would definitely reject the idea that he holds it for no reason or that it is unreasonable to hold it. But when asked for the evidence for such a belief, there is a certain difficulty. For in a sense the evidence for a belief of this kind is everything the man knows. He may indeed cite particular pieces of evidence. As Lewis says: "The man who accepts Christianity always thinks he has good evidence; whether, like Dante, *fisici e metafisici argoment*: or historical evidence, or the evidence of religious experience, or authority, or all of these together."[3] But, as Lewis has pointed out elsewhere, the Christian also accepts Christianity because it makes sense out of everything else he knows. And this is true also of the materialist, the Buddhist, and so on.

All world views or "fundamental faiths" have this characteristic: they "make sense of things" for those who accept

[2] Ibid.
[3] Ibid., p. 17.

them. But unless we are to accept pure relativism, one of these views must be true and the other false. One must *really* make sense of things and the others must only appear to. And to accept pure relativism is not to accept any world view at all, for if a view is no more true than any other view, it explains nothing at all.

Let us now consider some objections to the whole idea of faith. The objections can be listed as follows:

1. Faith is unreasonable, for it ignores evidence to the contrary.
2. Faith is unreasonable because it accepts what it does not fully understand.
3. Faith demands an unreasonable commitment; nothing can be worth the sacrifices it demands.
4. There can be no adequate reason for accepting any faith: our attitude should be one of proportioning belief to the evidence.

The first objection rests on a misunderstanding of what sort of "temptations against faith" the believer is urged to reject. The person who has faith does not believe there are any decisive arguments against his faith, and he will have no particular reason to search out such arguments unless he feels it his duty to seek out such objections to refute them. But he will have no fear of such arguments, nor will he have any objection to hearing, considering, and answering objections to his faith. He will, however, have to struggle against emotions that make him *feel* that his faith is false. Of course, this sort of thing occurs in a great many other cases also. Reason tells us that air travel is safer than most other means of transportation, but emotion makes us afraid to get on the plane. Experience tells us that anesthetics have worked in the past, but panic strikes us as the mask is lowered over our face. Anyone setting out on a marriage, a career, or a carefully thought-out and eminently worthwhile project has moments of despair, of panic, of loss of confidence. It is reason itself that tells us to ignore these feelings and carry on. And it is these emotional temptations against faith that we are recommended to resist.

There is also the fact that Christian faith is trust in a Person. To be suspicious, to seize on every excuse for doubt, to lack full confidence in the Person in whom we trust is a moral failure, just as it would be in the case of a trusted spouse or friend. As Lewis says:

> Our opponents, then, have a perfect right to dispute with us about the grounds of our original assent. But they must not accuse us of sheer insanity if, after the assent has been given, our adherence to it is no longer proportioned to every fluctuation in the apparent evidence. They cannot, of course, be expected to see how the *quality* of the object which we think we are beginning to know by acquaintance drives us to the view that if this were a delusion then we should have to say that the universe had produced no real thing of comparable value, and that all explanations of the delusion seemed somehow less important than the thing explained. That knowledge we cannot communicate. But they can see how the assent, of necessity, moves us from the logic of speculative thought into what perhaps might be called the logic of personal relations. What would, up til then, have been variations simply of opinion become variations of conduct by a person to a Person. *Credere Deum esse* turns into *Credere in Deum.* And *Deum* here is this God, the increasingly knowable Lord.[4]

This passage gives us some idea of the answer to the remaining objections. If our confidence is basically in a Person rather

[4] Ibid., pp. 29–30.

than in a set of propositions, then it is not unreasonable to believe what this Person tells us even if we do not completely understand it. We are, after all, in very much this position whenever we learn from someone wiser than ourselves. Because we have confidence in the person, we treat puzzling utterances as something worth working to understand. We do not reject whatever we cannot understand immediately. Some Christians who were trying to emphasize God's greatness have, indeed, talked as if we could understand nothing about God, and if this were true, our belief could have no content. But the case is, of course, that some things in the Christian message we understand immediately and easily, some things we come increasingly to understand as we try to live by them, and others remain dark to us in varying degrees. After all, there is nothing surprising in this. We have the same experience in reading a great philosopher or in getting to know another human being. The only things we can *completely* understand are very simple and abstract things like the laws of mechanics, or systems that have been invented by our own minds. But any real thing, even something as simple as a fish or an onion, is at least partly mysterious to us. Any completely comprehensible revelation would be immediately suspicious and probably man-made.

The third objection was that nothing can be worth the sort of commitment faith demands. This is important because it emphasizes that love as well as trust is a component of faith. Without hope and love, faith is not fully itself, just as love would be beggared without faith and trust. Any faith must contain some element of love and value, even if it is pure abstract love of truth or a love of the honesty that accepts unpleasant truths. And, of course, once love enters, it is impossible to say what sacrifices may not be demanded.

The final objection is that faith is a kind of madness; we should have no truck with total commitments of this sort but coolly proportion our belief to the sort of evidence we have. But, of course, this depends on the nature of the reality in which we have faith. If reality is an impersonal thing, or a set of impersonal things, total commitment to it is inappropriate, just as total commitment to clothes or fast cars or model trains is inappropriate. Things neither demand nor properly receive total commitment. But if the reality we believe in is ultimately personal, then a total commitment may be the only appropriate response. Faith is part of our total response to that Reality, and if Christianity is right, then total faith, total trust, and total love are what is asked of us. Whether Christianity *is* right we will explore in the following chapters.

7

The Nature of the Universe

Christians, along with Muslims and some other religious groups, believe in the existence of a personal Being who created the universe. If what we said about religious belief in the last chapter is true, then there should be some reason for holding this belief. In this chapter, we shall look at the main reasons philosophers and other people have found for belief in God. These reasons are often discussed separately, but we shall consider them as parts of one argument, which I think is the best way of looking at them. If, as I believe, these reasons need to be considered together as part of a single argument, then the usual tactic of considering each of them as a separate argument and criticizing them on that basis may be a tactic of "divide and conquer". It is easy to show that no part of the engine taken separately can move the car, but working together, these parts *can* move the car.

Another preliminary point to be aware of is this: many treatments of arguments for God's existence take some very old and very short treatment of the proofs for God's existence and then follow this with later criticisms, some written by present-day philosophers. Now, even if the old version of the argument is essentially correct, as it may be, the impression given (sometimes, I fear, intentionally) is that of a historical progression: long ago, this is how men thought they could argue for God's existence, but then such-and-such criticisms were discovered. But in fact, both arguments and objections have been long debated. Also, the language used and the assumptions made by an older philosophical text create difficulties in understanding and appreciating the argument.

A particular favorite for this tactic is the version of five arguments for God's existence given by Saint Thomas Aquinas in a very long work, which was a sort of philosophical and theological encyclopedia, called the *Summa Theologica*. This version covers only about a page of print and was never intended as a full-scale version of the arguments, only as a sort of reminder for those who knew them already. It was addressed to philosophers who might or might not be Christians but who agreed with Aquinas about certain ways of doing philosophy and certain philosophical positions, mostly derived from the Greek philosopher Aristotle. Terms like *cause* and *motion* are used in senses that are no longer familiar. This is all to the advantage of those who want a good brief statement of the arguments so that they can proceed to their real business of refuting them. But a philosopher who wants to defend this type of argument should choose a better ground for his defense.

Let us begin by considering a question most people have thought of at one time or another: How did the universe as we know it begin (if it did begin)? There are essentially three possible answers to this question:

1. The universe simply popped into existence, after a period in which nothing at all existed.
2. The universe as we know it, that is, a universe composed mainly of material objects scattered throughout

space, has always existed, although it may have changed in many ways.

3. The universe of material objects in space began to exist at some time and was brought into existence by something nonmaterial and nonspatial.

The real choice, of course, is between the second and third alternatives, for hardly anyone takes the first alternative seriously. Because it will be useful later, we will briefly see why the first alternative is so implausible. One thing we could say about the possibility of the universe simply coming into existence from nothing is to declare that "nothing comes from nothing." There is not just a factual impossibility involved, like the impossibility of flapping your arms and flying to the moon, but a kind of *logical* impossibility. We can make a mental picture of something simply "popping" into existence, but we cannot really make sense of the idea.

But suppose that someone denies the inconceivability of something coming from nothing. What can we say to him? We can, of course, challenge him to cite an instance of something coming from nothing, and if he does so, he may reveal a misunderstanding of what he is denying. He may, for example, cite the theory of "continuous creation" held by some scientific cosmologists. But this theory does not claim that matter comes into existence from nothing but says that in certain areas of space, matter is formed from energy, rather as drops of dew condense from water vapor. Even if this theory were true, it would no more contradict the principle that nothing comes from nothing than it would contradict the "creation" of dewdrops from water vapor.

Suppose, however, that the denial did not rest on a misunderstanding and that the objector seriously maintained that things can just pop into existence for no reason at all. We could point out that if this happened at the beginning of the universe, there would be no reason why it should not happen now. We could point out that no one would take seriously the idea that anything—a baseball, a planet, even a snowflake—had simply popped into existence from nothing. The impossibility of this sort of thing is a basic assumption of any coherent thinking about the universe. For if any explanation of the existence of any particular thing may be just "it popped into existence for no reason", and if the ultimate explanation of everything is just that, then all explanation is undermined. So to hold the "pop" theory of the origin of the universe is to give up any hope of rationality or understandability in the universe. If someone claims to hold this view, then he cannot be reached by rational argument, for he has abandoned rationality. But if someone abandons rationality, he can have no reason for holding any view and no reason for action except momentary passion or appetite. He has, in effect, stepped out of the human race down to the animal level. This is a solution of sorts to some problems, but then so is suicide.

The second alternative is not on the face of it open to the same sort of objection. It seems to be logically possible for A to be caused by B, for B to be caused by C, and so on, backward ad infinitum. There is, however, a very serious objection to this sort of "infinite regress", as it is called.

Consider any series where A depends on B, B depends on C, and so on. We can describe such series in a general way by saying that they are cases where A has a certain property (that is, a certain thing, a certain quality, etc.) only if B has it, B has it only if C has it, and so on. For example, if A tries to borrow a lawn mower from B, and B replies, "I don't have one, but I'll borrow one from my friend C", and C says, "I don't have one, but I'll borrow one from my friend D", and so on, this is a case of the kind we are concerned with. Or if A asks B, his supervisor, for permission to take the afternoon off and B says, "I can't give you permission without asking my supervisor, C", and C says, "I can't give you permission to give A permission unless I ask my supervisor, D", and so on, we have a case of this sort.

Now in these ordinary cases, two things are clear:

1. If the series of things that do not have the property in question goes on to infinity, the first individual never gets that property. If *everyone* asked says, "I don't have a lawn mower, but I'll ask . . .", A never gets his lawn mower. If *every* supervisor asked says, "I can't give you permission, but I'll ask . . .", then A never gets his afternoon off.

2. If the first thing *does* get the property in question, then the series came to an end and did *not* go on to infinity. If A gets his lawn mower, someone along the line had a lawn mower without having to borrow one. If A gets his afternoon off, some supervisor could give permission without having to ask someone else.

Now, there may be something special about these cases that prevents these two points from being generalized to all cases of dependent series. For example, both cases go *forward* in time—first A asks B, then B asks C, and so on. Also, both cases involve situations having natural limits: there are not an infinite number of people who can be asked for the loan of a lawn mower; no company has an infinite number of supervisors.

So let us consider general cases where these limitations do not seem to apply. Suppose that A, B, C, etc., are actions or states and the property in question is desirability. A is jogging, and it is desirable for the sake of B, which is loss of weight, which is desirable for the sake of C, which is health, and so on. But if this series goes on to infinity, how can we say that A is desirable? (Aristotle used an argument just like this to show that some things must be desired for their own sake and not for the sake of something else.)

Another example is definition: if I define word A in terms of word B, then A is understandable only if B is. But if B is understandable only if C is, and so on, then either we never understand A at all or we come to some word that is understood without being defined by another word. (Thus, Aristotle argued, not every word can be defined.)

Or in terms of proof, if A is a statement that can be proved only if B is proved, and B can be proved only if C is, and so on, then either A is never proved at all or else we come to some statement that is known to be true without being proved by another statement. (Aristotle argued that there were two kinds of such statements: descriptions of immediate experience, and self-evident truths.)

Now let us apply this general pattern to the existence of particular things. My existence, for example, depends on the existence of my parents, their existence on the existence of their parents, and so on. Eventually we come to a human being or human beings whose existence must be accounted for by some cause other than procreation by other humans, but whatever the details of this series, it is evidently a case of a dependent series. And if so, then it would seem that if the series was an infinite regress, I would not exist, and since I do exist, the series must have had a beginning. What sort of beginning? Plainly, a thing that exists whether or not anything else exists, for nothing else would put an end to a series of this kind. A being that exists whether or not anything else exists would, of course, always exist. A being of this kind is traditionally called a *necessary* being. Thus, if we can rule out an infinite regress in the realm of existence, we arrive at the existence of a necessary being, a being that always exists whether anything else exists or not, just as in previous arguments we reached the existence of a statement that is true whether or not it is proved by any other true statement, a word that can be understood whether or not it is defined by any other word, a state that is desired whether or not any other state was desired, a supervisor who could give permission whether or not anyone gave him permission, and a man who had a lawn mower whether or not anyone loaned him one. If there is something different about the existence case, it is not obvious what it is.

Now of course God, as pictured by traditional Christianity, is a necessary Being; he exists whether or not anything else exists, and he always exists. So if we can prove the existence of a necessary being, we have made a step toward proving the existence of God, just as if we were trying to prove the existence of intelligent life on Mars, we would have made a step forward if we were to prove the existence of life on Mars.

But have we proved the existence of a necessary being? It is clear enough that any series of causes is a dependent series, for part of what we mean by saying that A was caused by B is that A would not have existed unless B had. It is clear enough that in almost any other dependent series we can think of, the two principles we have discussed apply. Thus, to deny that they apply to the case of causes is to be inconsistent, unless we can show that this case is different from the others in some way. To be inconsistent, to say that a principle applies in one case but not in another case that is similar in all relevant respects, is to abandon reason. So we must either find a difference in the causal case or deny that the principles apply to any case. The second course would be unreasonable, but it would not have the same disastrous effects on our reasoning that accepting the "pop" theory would.

However, it might be claimed that the second group of cases *are* all cases that go forward in time. "All that your argument proves", it might be claimed, "is that if we try to explain A by B, B by C, and so on, we would never reach the end of the explanation. But this is all right, since each thing in the series would have an explanation." There are several replies to this. First, it is not clear that any of the cases really depends on the direction in time. If, before trying to borrow the lawn mower, A is told that *no one* has a lawn mower unless he can borrow one, he knows he will never get a mower. If a company is set up in such a way that no supervisor can give permission without asking it, we know that no permissions will be given. But some of the later cases give us another aspect of the matter. Take the definition case. Suppose you are reading J. R. R. Tolkien's *Lord of the Rings* and you come across the dwarvish word *uzbad*. I explain to you that it means the same as the elvish word *aran*. This is no help, since you know no more of elvish than you do of dwarvish. If I continue giving you words in unknown languages as definitions, then you never understand the word with which we started. Now, if I ask why the universe as it is now, or something in it, exists, and you answer my question by showing that it was caused by a previously existing thing or state of the universe about which exactly the same question can be raised, has my original question really been answered?

As for the idea that "each thing in the series will have an explanation", this would be equally true if our explanations were circular, that is, if we explained A by B, B by C, and C by A. If we gave a circular definition, defining *uzbad* by *aran* and *aran* by *uzbad*, we could say "each word has a definition." But this is obviously unsatisfactory, so the mere fact that "each thing in the series has an explanation" does not mean we have a satisfactory answer to our first question. But it is important to remember that the argument was in terms of existence, not in terms of explanation of existence: unless the argument is mistaken, if there is an infinite regress of causes, I do not exist; and since the same argument can be applied to anything, nothing exists—which is absurd.

However, it is possible to reject the conclusion that a necessary being must exist without, seemingly, rejecting reason. We can say that there is something different about this case even though we cannot put our finger on it. We can say that the impossibility of infinite regress in the other cases is due to some special features of those cases. So if someone is not convinced by the argument, there seems to be an impasse.

Let us try to avoid this impasse by going ahead a bit on the assumption that a necessary being does exist and asking what sort of being this would be. Could the necessary being just be the material universe itself? No, for the material universe is just a collection of things none of which is necessary, and the property of always existing whether or not anything else exists is not the sort of property that can be reached by simply adding things together that lack this property. We can get a thing that weighs a ton by adding together lots of things that do not weigh a ton, but we cannot get a thing that is transparent by adding together any number of things that are not transparent. In cases where we can get a property by adding, we get nearer to it by even small additions: two things that weigh a pound each put together are *nearer* a ton than either separately. But two opaque things together are no more transparent than either separately, and two things that exist only because other things do are no nearer existing necessarily together than apart.

Could the necessary being be the basic "stuff" of the universe? Suppose that it were. This would solve one of our difficulties, since it would answer the question as to why anything exists at all. The answer would be that the basic stuff of the universe (matter, energy, or whatever it is) exists whether or not anything else exists. But it would not answer the question as to why any particular thing, for example, you or me or the planet we live on, exists. To explain this without bringing in God, we would have to fall back on one of the theories we mentioned in chapter 3. The existence of particular things would have to be explained by chance combinations of the basic stuff, or by some "natural necessity" somehow built into that stuff. But as we saw in chapter 3, either answer is fatal to reason. If either of these answers is true, we could not know that it is, or that anything else is.

Now that we have reached this point, we can see that the infinite regress theory is open to the same objection. Even if the general answer to the question, "Why does anything exist?" is "Because something existed at some previous time", this does not give us an answer to the question, "Why do the particular things that exist now exist?" To say that it is because certain particular things existed at a previous time and that certain causal laws operated to bring about the present state of affairs is simply to push the difficulty back to the previous states of affairs and the laws.

We are faced, in fact, with a problem about the nature of the universe as experience reveals it. We see that the universe behaves in a regular and broadly predictable way, and we can understand many of the regularities and use them to predict and control events. The universe, in other words, is *orderly* and *intelligible*. This orderliness and intelligibility must be explainable in one of three ways:

1. As the result of design by a mind in some ways like ours.
2. As the result of chance.
3. As the result of "natural necessity".

We have already seen the difficulties inherent in the last two possibilities. But there are additional drawbacks. Consider the problems we face in decoding any apparently intelligible message, for example, one of Tolkien's elvish or runic inscriptions. If we believe that the message is the result of intelligent design and is meant to be decoded, then we can have some hope of finding a pattern that makes sense. But if the apparent message is the result of mere chance throwing together of lines, then not only can we not expect any apparent regularities we have encountered to continue, but the supposed regularities we think we have discovered are illusory. So the result of accepting the chance theory in a consistent way would be the expectation that natural laws might cease to operate any second and the realization that all of our apparent scientific knowledge was illusory, because there were no real regularities, only "runs of luck" or patterns we had read into the chance variations of nature.

Even on the "natural necessity" theory, the same difficulty threatens. Some of Tolkien's runes look rather like trees: suppose that the runic "inscription" turned out just to be a simplified picture of the trees in front of Tolkien's house. What confidence could we have that any supposed message we read into the runes was really there or that trees at the side of the house would continue the supposed message? But on the natural necessity view, any regularities in the universe might for all we know have as little in common with our minds as the growth of branches on a tree. In fact, of course, if we found that there was a message in the way the trees were shaped, we would immediately suspect intelligent interference: someone must have trained or pruned the trees to carry the message. In talking about *parts* of the universe, we never assume that intelligible order "just grew".

Thus again we have a contrast of two possible views of the universe. On the theistic view the material universe is caused by an intelligent necessary being, and this explains not only its existence but its order and intelligibility. On the "pop" theory, the universe is meaningless and reason is useless. On the view that the basic stuff of the universe is necessary, we have an explanation of sorts of the *existence* of the universe but not of its orderliness and intelligibility. And on the infinite regress theory, even if we can get over its other difficulties, we also have no explanation for the orderliness and intelligibility of the universe. We have to supplement the theory with either the chance theory or the natural necessity theory, and both have fatal difficulties.

Thus we begin to see what Lewis meant by saying he accepted the Christian view because it made sense of everything else. The view that the universe was created by God seems to be the only view that accounts for all the facts: it gives reason a place and leads us to expect continued regularity and understandability in the universe.

Two objections may occur to you here. The first is the old difficulty, "Who made God?" But if God is a necessary being, then the question has no point: no one made God; he always existed and always will, no matter what else exists or does not exist. We can also see that the usual objection to this reply, "Then why not say the universe always existed and always will, no matter what else does or doesn't exist?" can be answered by what we have already said. If by the "universe" we mean just the collection of nonnecessary things, lumping them together does not make them necessary. If we mean "the basic stuff of the universe" then we are left without an explanation of orderliness and intelligibility. Of course, we could combine the theories, saying that God and the basic stuff of the universe have *both* always existed, God accounting for orderliness and intelligibility. But why posit two necessary beings when one will do the job? (There are also objections to the idea of a number of independent necessary beings. What is their supposed relation? How would they affect each other?)

Of course, there are objections that can be made to the arguments and answers to these objections, and so on. That is why philosophy is best done in a living dialogue, where objections can be stated and answered as they come up.

8

The Nature of Morality

If the conclusions of the last chapter are correct, then the only explanation of the existence and nature of the universe that makes sense of what we know about the universe is that it is brought into existence by an intelligent Being, who has always existed and who exists whether or not anything else exists. Obviously, such a Being has something in common with the Jewish and Christian and Muslim idea of God. But we are still a long way from the full idea of such a Being that we find in these religions. We have not yet given any evidence for the existence of a *"righteous* Jehovah", a *"just* and *merciful* Allah", a "God the *Father"*. To do so, we must return to the moral theories discussed in chapter 4. If there is no moral law, or if the moral law is independent of God, then the Power that explains the existence and intelligibility of the universe need not be good. But if the moral law exists and has its origin in the same Power that explains the existence and intelligibility of the universe, then we have at least arrived at a just and righteous God if not yet a merciful or loving God.

If we can show that an objective moral law exists and that the only reasonable explanation of the existence of this objective moral law is that it has its origin in a personal

Being, and that this Being is the same as the Being who accounts for the order and intelligibility of the universe, then we will have come much closer to proving the existence of God in the full sense. To do this, we must briefly consider possible objections to each of these points and then examine the positive arguments.

The main objection to the notion that there is an objective moral law is the seeming widespread disagreement about moral rules. Of course, disagreement about particular cases is no evidence for disagreement about moral *rules*, for differences in factual belief may account for disagreement about cases. But if two people agree about all the facts at issue and disagree about particular cases, this may mean that they disagree about moral rules; and if they understand a moral rule in the same way and if one accepts it and the other rejects it, then there is straightforward disagreement about moral rules.

What needs to be shown then, if this objection to the idea of objective moral law is to work, is that people do in fact disagree about moral rules and that disagreement does in fact show that there is no objective moral law. Neither is as easy to show as some have thought.

Let us first look at what might plausibly be meant by an objective moral law, and second, at what agreement we might reasonably expect to find about it.

It is important to begin with the idea of a person. We ordinarily regard the killing of an animal differently from the killing of a human being because we ordinarily regard human beings, but not animals, as persons. Those who object to the killing of animals are very often those who for one reason or another regard animals as persons or quasi persons. Primitive tribes may regard treachery, torture, etc., of non-members of the tribe as justified at least partly because they do not regard anyone outside the tribe as really being a person. Slave-owning societies can survive only by not regarding slaves as persons, and racial or sexual prejudice survives at least partly by refusal to regard the group discriminated against as real persons. What we call "advances" or "progress" in morality occur largely when people not previously regarded as persons come to be regarded as persons.

Another important source of confusion about morality arises from differences in the way certain commitments are regarded. If marriage is regarded as a lifelong, exclusive commitment, one sort of behavior will be expected; if it is regarded as temporary or nonexclusive, another sort will be appropriate. Thus, for example, to say that one society regards revolution against the established government as right, and another regards it is wrong, can be misleading, unless both societies regard their commitment to government in the same way.

There may also be disagreement about just what responsibilities rest on a person. In some societies, for example, a maternal uncle has the responsibilities a father has in our society; in others, the responsibility of a child to parents is greater or less than in our society, and so on.

Given this clarification, we can now make our claim clear. I want to claim that in every society, men have recognized responsibilities and commitments to other persons, have regarded certain actions toward persons as right and others as wrong, regardless of whether or not these actions were in their own interest or not. Furthermore, there is general, although not perfect, agreement on specific obligations. Differences about specific obligations that cannot be explained as differences in factual beliefs can largely be traced to differences as to who is a person, or as to the nature of a commitment, or as to the locus of a responsibility.

This, I maintain, is what might reasonably be expected if there is an objective moral law. A good parallel is the case of logic. There is broad general agreement on what arguments are good or bad ones. People will make different judgments about specific arguments because of factual disagreements about truth of premises, because they disagree about the scope or application of general principles, etc. But there is not a Chinese logic, a European logic, an African logic in the sense of different and incompatible principles. There are different ways of systematizing logic, just as there are different systematizations of morality, but these rest on a basis of common agreement as to goodness or badness of general types of argument.

Presumably most people would agree that this is the case with regard to logic, for if there is not one standard of logical correctness for all men, then no argument can be trusted. But if the diversity we find about morality is no different in kind than the diversity we find about logical arguments, then if the diversity in one case does not disprove the objectivity of the laws of logic, the diversity in the other case does not disprove the objectivity of the moral law.

Our positive reasons for believing in the existence of an objective moral law grow directly out of these considerations. Just as, if we are to argue at all, we must assume the truth of certain logical principles, so if we are to judge on any basis other than that of pure self-interest, we must assume certain moral principles. To judge purely on the basis of our own self-interest is theoretically possible, just as it is theoretically possible to have only pragmatic considerations in argument, and care nothing about truth. But in practice, no one can do either. We want to know the truth even if it does not "pay off", and we need to make moral judgments even if they are against our own interest. We can fail to act morally and still be human, but to lose the capacity to distinguish between the moral and the immoral is to lose our humanity. In Ibsen's *Peer Gynt*, Peer will cheerfully lie about what he sees, but he refuses to become a troll by losing his capacity to tell the difference between truth and falsity. So, also, to lose our capacity to make moral distinctions is to become, if not trolls, then at least not men.

The claim of moral nihilism is sometimes made by people in our society, frequently in an effort to escape from guilt in matters of sexual morality, etc. But it is noticeable that as soon as something occurs outside the area in which they feel personal guilt, these people immediately apply the language of moral judgment with great vigor and often with compensatory exaggeration. Some men seem to make no judgments except those of personal advantage: they are moral solipsists who if unsuccessful are criminals but if successful may be tyrants or tycoons. But even they cannot totally escape from the making of moral judgments, if they are sane.

There is, of course, a long and complicated argument involved in establishing the existence of an objective moral law. It involves factual matters (how great, in fact, is variation in moral *standards*?) and logical ones (what does variation prove?). The subject is simply too large to take up here, but there are good arguments against relativism and for an objective moral law.[1] For the moment, at any rate, we must take it that the existence of an objective moral law can be proved along the lines indicated and go on to our second task.

This, you will remember, was to show that a personal Being is the origin of the moral law. The usual objection to this runs as follows:

---

[1] A good introductory book on this subject is C. S. Lewis' *Abolition of Man* (San Francisco: Harper, 2001).

A God who was a moral lawgiver would either have to judge moral goodness or badness by some standard independent of himself, in which case we could appeal to this standard without reference to him, or he would decide goodness or badness in a purely arbitrary way. But if this were true, God might have made cruelty good and kindness evil, which is morally absurd. Thus considerations about God's will are morally irrelevant.

As we said in chapter 4, there is an element of misunderstood truth in this claim. The truth involved is that if God were merely powerful without also being good, it would be our duty to do what is good whether or not God willed it. But if we reflect on the argument, we soon see that the idea of a morality existing somehow "in the nature of things", where the "things" are nonpersonal and nonrational, is as open to objections as the idea of an objective natural law without a rational Being as its origin.

What could it mean to say that there was an objective morality in the nature of things? That human beings have beliefs that certain kinds of action are right or wrong? But what about the universe before human beings existed? Was there or was there not a right and wrong then? And if we say there was, what do we mean? If the beliefs were implanted in us by the workings of nonrational forces, what reason do we have to trust them? Surely an intelligent lemming feeling a deep sense of rightness about rushing into the sea with his fellow lemmings would be well advised to criticize and reject the belief, would he not? How can it be rational to obey a moral belief that is simply the result of chance or of the working of mindless forces?

Are we then flung on the other horn of the dilemma? Does God merely decide arbitrarily what will be right and wrong? As we saw briefly in chapter 4, the answer is no. The laws of morality, like the laws of reason, are the laws of God's own nature. God cannot act irrationally, nor can he act immorally, for he cannot act against his own nature. We can act irrationally or immorally, for it is left to our own choice whether we will conform to reason, to physical reality, or to moral reality.

But, it might be objected, if morality can be the law of God's nature, why cannot we eliminate God and say that it is merely the law of *our* nature? Because God's nature is what it is whether or not anything else exists and whatever else happens. But our natures are contingent: if our rationality and morality do not come from God, they come from chance permutations of some basic stuff or from the working of mindless forces. In either case, they have no validity.

Also, our moral experience is not just an experience of feeling certain moral obligations but of feeling these obligations *and* failing to live up to them. Just as errors in beliefs are a problem for any theory that tries to explain human reason as merely the working out of inherent laws, so moral failure or error is a problem for any theory of a morality inherent in the nature of the universe. Again, how could we feel guilt toward, or responsibility to, a nonpersonal law? Thus, if there is an objective moral law, as there seems to be, it can only be rational to obey this law if it has its origin in a Person. Of course, it might be prudent to obey the arbitrary decrees of a powerful God whose commandments were based only on whim, but it can only be *moral* to obey a God whose nature is goodness.

Finally, let us consider the question as to whether the Person who is the source of morality is the same as the Person who is the source of the order and intelligibility of the universe. Why not postulate two entities? it might be asked. But even just on grounds of simplicity, there seems no need to "multiply entities without reason". Further-more, our reason seems to grasp both logical and moral laws: if a different origin is to be postulated for these two, why not a different origin for deductive and inductive reason, or for mathematical and nonmathematical laws? Thus, I think no one who has agreed with us thus far will take seriously the possibility that one personal Being is the origin of reason and another of morality.

If our reasoning so far is correct, then the Person responsible for the existence and intelligibility of the universe is also responsible for our moral judgments. Thus the only reasonable explanation for two basic areas of our experience, reasoning and making moral judgments, is the existence of a Person who begins to look more and more like the God of traditional theism.

Can we go further, to the existence of the loving and merciful God of Christianity? Here we are on more questionable ground. I suspect that unaided human reason would at best arrive at a God of justice, rather like the Stoic conception of God at its best. A god of perfect fairness—but, as Hamlet said, "If each of us had his deserts, who should escape whipping?" Also, the present muddled and miserable state of mankind would create some problems even for the notion of a just God.

Christianity provides two necessary answers here: an answer to the problem of why we are in our present mess, and an answer to the problem of how we are to think of the justice of God without despair. The idea of some original catastrophe—the much-abused and misunderstood idea of Original Sin—is surely a hypothesis that recommends itself to reason. There must be some explanation for the difference between our ideals and our performance, between our aspirations and our actions. And the idea that God himself has taken a hand in repairing this original catastrophe is surely, when properly understood, the best possible solution to our worries about God's justice. This does not in itself show that it is the true solution, but surely Tolkien ought to be right in saying that "there is no tale told which men would rather find was true." If he is not right, it is either because the problem is not seen or felt or because the solution is not understood.

Thus I conclude that reason takes us as far as the idea of a just and righteous God and therefore shows us a problem to which the Christian message is the natural solution. To reject the notion of a Person whose nature is the foundation of morality is ultimately to rob the notion of morality of any meaning. To do this is to give up any right to praise or blame, to call any action evil or any man good. And to do this is to become a troll rather than a man. Remove God from the universe and man does not step up to the empty throne but instead steps down to the level of the beasts.

9

The Nature of Happiness

It is often claimed that there is a special area of experience that can be explained only by the action of God, what is sometimes called "religious experience". Unfortunately, discussion of it is often sidetracked into a discussion of mystical experience, and genuine mystical experience seems to be as rare and as hard to pin down as authentic genius. I am willing to grant that if you are a great mystic, or even if you know such a person, you may have experiences for which the special action of God is the only reasonable explanation. But this is so far from the experience of most of us as to be of very little use for our present purposes. Thus I want to concentrate on a much more common experience, a certain kind of happiness or longing for happiness that most of us have experienced in one way or another. First we must look briefly at the nature of happiness.

A man may be said to be happy in three senses:

(a) if he has no unsatisfied desires;
(b) if he is actively enjoying some good thing;
(c) if he is doing what he wants to be doing.

I will call sense (a) *contentment*, sense (b) *enjoying yourself*, and sense (c) *doing what you choose*. It is clear that you can be contented without enjoying yourself; some apathetic people seem to have no enjoyment in their lives yet seem to desire nothing. You can be enjoying something even though you have unsatisfied desires, like a man enjoying a mystery story on a plane en route to reunion with a loved one. You can do what you choose without being either contented or enjoying yourself, like the man who by his own choice sacrifices his life for a cause. Whether you can be contented or be enjoying yourself without in one sense doing what you choose is less clear. But it seems that you can have contentment without enjoyment, have enjoyment without contentment, and do what you choose without either.

Even these simple distinctions can help us resolve some elementary confusions. If someone claims that no one voluntarily acts except in order to obtain happiness, this is obviously false for senses (a) and (b), for many people act in ways they know will not give them happiness in the sense of contentment or enjoyment (for example, the man going to prison for a cause he believes in). Sense (c) is open to two interpretations. If we mean "doing what you in fact choose", then the proposed principle is just that if you act voluntarily you are doing what you in fact choose, which of course is true by definition. If we mean "doing what you would prefer to do", then again the principle is false, for many people do things they would prefer not to do. Thus the principle is either trivially true by definition or false.

We can be sure of contentment by having no desires, and reasonably sure of contentment by having no desires that we are unable to satisfy. Philosophical Buddhism recommends the first course, Stoicism the second. If death is extinction, then the dead are happy in the sense of being content.

By ordinary reckoning, no one can be sure of happiness in the sense of continuous enjoyment or in the sense of always doing what we prefer to do. We can always do what we choose to do if we choose whatever in fact we find ourselves doing, but this is a rather Pickwickian sense of "doing what we choose". Epicureanism recommends the careful cultivation of available and uncostly pleasures, and both Epicureanism and Stoicism, for rather different reasons, recommend resignation to what cannot be helped. If death is extinction, then the dead are not happy in the sense of enjoying themselves or doing what they choose.

Perfect happiness, presumably, would be happiness in all three senses, total enjoyment with no unsatisfied desires and doing always what we prefer to do. Such happiness no one has claimed to find in this life. Even the greatest enjoyment lasts for a limited time and with repetition tends to be less enjoyable. Contentment by extinction of desires is not perfect happiness, and contentment that depends on certain desires being satisfied can and will always be destroyed by some circumstance that prevents the desire being satisfied. Even the most fortunate of men eventually grows old and dies. There is even less security in happiness based on doing as we choose, since for any being who is less than omnipotent, there will always be frustrations. Thus perfect happiness always eludes us, and the man who thinks he will attain it by pursuing pleasure or riches or power is ignoring the universal testimony of history.

Yet all men desire perfect happiness. If the universe were absurd or meaningless, if there were no rationality or understandability in the universe, this unsatisfied longing might only be a cruel mischance. But if the conclusions of the last two chapters are correct, then there are order and intelligibility, a law of reason and a moral law that we cannot escape. If we live in a rational universe, there must be some reason for our longing for personal happiness, and if the Source of the natural law is also the Source of the moral law, then this desire cannot be a cruel trick.

Men have, of course, sometimes talked as if God could be actually evil or at least indifferent to good and evil. On this view, even if the moral law is given to *us* by God, *he* may not act according to it. But there are unsurmountable difficulties in this view. If God is good, then there can be a reasonable explanation of the existence of evil, as we have seen. But if God is evil or indifferent, how can the existence of good be explained? A completely evil being would have no reason for creating all the sources of joy and gladness that are in the world—colors, tastes, delights, friendships, accomplishments. A God who was indifferent to good and evil would have no motive for giving man a moral code. If our reasons for believing in God are good ones, then God must be a Being who exists and has a certain nature whether anything else exists or not. Thus he could have nothing to gain from making men behave in a certain way. An earthly tyrant may impose a code of conduct to make himself secure or to obtain certain services. But God can neither be harmed nor helped by the creatures he has made.

A God who is purely good, who created us for our own happiness, is conceivable. It might seem at first glance that a purely evil God is a possibility. But once we look at the nature of evil, we see that this is not a real possibility. Evil in our experience arises from selfishness, with its consequent desire to use others, to treat people as means to our own satisfaction. But God cannot need to use others in this way: a purely selfish God would presumably not create anything at all, for nothing is needful to God.

Some might say that we know so little of God that we can form no idea of what he would or would not do. But the very reasons we have for believing in God's existence at all give us grounds for knowing something about him. He must be at least as intelligent as the most intelligent being we can conceive of and at least as good as the best person we can conceive of, for our reason and our morality both come from him.

So we find that only the existence of a just and reasonable God can give us any hope of perfect happiness, and since we obviously lack such happiness here and now, we must expect it after death. Does this lead to the conclusion that our belief in God is wish fulfillment? No, for, as we have seen, if a just God exists, we are responsible to him. Again, perfect happiness is promised to us not unconditionally but only if we do what we can to earn it. (Not that, on the Christian view, we can really deserve perfect happiness; but even if it is a gift beyond our deserts, we should want to deserve it as much as we can.)

There is also, even in this life, an experience of happiness or longing for happiness that many of us have experienced in one way or another. In his autobiographical sketch *Surprised by Joy*, C. S. Lewis described how this experience, which he called "Joy", led him eventually to accept theism and later to accept Christianity.[1] This feeling of delight and longing, poignantly described by Lewis, seemed inexplicable to him when he was an agnostic. He tried to identify it with sexual longing, with aesthetic pleasure, and so on, but experience showed that none of these explanations was sufficient. Finally the only way Lewis could explain this experience of "Joy" was as a foretaste of the happiness

[1] *Surprised by Joy* (Harvest Books / Harcourt, 2001), see especially p. 200.

promised to man by God, and a beckoning toward that happiness.

Whether or not we feel the experience of "Joy" as keenly as Lewis felt it or are able to describe it as well as he could, most of us have had an experience of a longing for happiness that no earthly happiness can satisfy. Of course, a longing for something does not prove that we will get that thing or even that such a thing exists. But if the universe makes sense at all, a longing for something should be a clue to a need in our nature that can somehow be met. As Lewis says:

> Creatures are not born with desires unless satisfaction for those desires exists. A baby feels hunger: well, there is such a thing as food. A duckling wants to swim: well, there is such a thing as water. Men feel sexual desire: well, there is such a thing as sex. If I find in myself a desire which no experience in this world can satisfy, the most probable explanation is that I was made for another world. If none of my earthly pleasures satisfy it, that does not prove that the universe is a fraud. Probably earthly pleasures were never meant to satisfy it, but to arouse it, to suggest the real thing.[2]

We *can* reject this line of reasoning and say that our desire for a happiness that no earthly happiness can satisfy is a mere accident or fraud. But if it is not a mere accident or fraud, then it is another clue or pointer to the nature of the Source from which reality comes. God is not only the Source of the order and intelligibility of the universe and the Source of the moral law, but he is also the Source of our longing for perfect happiness.

We can reject all these lines of argument, but at a cost. As we have seen, if God is not the Source of reason, then

---

[2] *Mere Christianity* (San Francisco: Harper, 2001), pp. 136–39.

we cannot be sure reason has any relevance to the universe. If God is not the Source of morality, then there is no objective moral law that can make demands on all men, and we are left with our subjective likes and dislikes, or with moral ideas programmed into us by a mindless nature and therefore without foundation. Similarly, in this case we see that we can reject the idea of a God who holds out a promise of perfect happiness. But if we do so, we reduce the longing for perfect happiness to an accident or a deception.

Thus a universe without God is a universe without reason, a universe without moral values, a universe without hope of lasting happiness. It is precisely this world that the modern atheist or agnostic inhabits, precisely this world that the modern theater of the absurd, novel of the absurd, art of the absurd, shout, whine, and snivel about. If reason left us no alternative to such a view, intellectual honesty might force us to accept it. But if this view is true, reason has no force. If morality impelled us to take such a view, integrity might make us choose it. But if the view is true, morality has no force. If the deepest needs of our nature were satisfied by this view, then our nature might compel us to accept it. But if this view is true, the deepest needs of our nature are illusory. In sum, there can be no reason for accepting the absurdist view of the universe, for that view destroys all reasons.

All these arguments apply to both the theist and the nontheist. But what many religious believers would cite as an "argument from religious experience" is their own feelings of peace and joy that derive from their religious belief. The difficulty in using this as an argument addressed to those who lack religious belief is the problem of how one person's experience can be evidence for another person. If, for example, you are thinking of studying philosophy and I tell you that I derive deep satisfaction from teaching and studying philosophy, does this prove that you will derive the same satisfaction? Suppose you undertake a long course of study and find that philosophy is not your "cup of tea". The hesitations you may feel can be listed under several headings:

1. Doubts about whether I am self-deceived. For example, you may reflect that I have an investment of many years in my philosophical career; perhaps I am kidding myself about the satisfaction I feel in that career.

2. Doubts about whether our needs, desires, etc., are sufficiently alike for my experience to be a guide for you. For example, you may feel that you are more adventurous than I and would be bored by an academic life or that you are more luxury-loving and couldn't live on an academic salary.

3. Doubts about whether there may not be some greater source of satisfaction unknown to me. For example, you may know that I have never been a talk show host, an advertising executive, an acid freak, or a Trappist monk, and you may wonder whether one of those careers may not bring greater happiness than philosophy.

I may be quite sure that I am not self-deceived, and some situation where I am given a real chance at some other career may prove my satisfaction with the life of a philosopher. But I cannot, in the nature of the case, settle your doubts about your unlikeness to myself or about other sources of satisfaction that I have not tried.

In the case of the peace and happiness that religious belief brings, some evidence is available to us to settle doubts of these three kinds. Doubts about whether religious believers are self-deluded about the happiness their belief brings can at least partly be answered by the many instances in which this happiness has persisted despite circumstances that remove all natural sources of satisfaction. Saint Francis, exuberant in his poverty; Saint Ignatius of Antioch, joyful on his way to death in the arena; and many ordinary Christians suffering all kinds of deprivations with serenity are all evidence of this kind. Such experiences are common and well attested.

We can, of course, persist in the diagnosis of self-delusion or propose psychiatric explanations of one kind or another. But this is not very plausible in many cases. Neuroses and psychoses do not in general lead to joy or serenity, and joy and serenity are generally based on specific physical or mental conditions. When all the usual physical or mental conditions of joy or serenity are absent and when the sanity and balance of a mind are evident, then to explain serenity or joy psychiatrically or as self-delusions may merely mark a refusal to consider the obvious religious explanation.

The difficulty about differences between persons can at least partly be answered by looking at the wide variety of persons who have derived happiness from religious belief. In fact, if we do not beg the question by building some reference to religious belief into our definition of the class, there is no class of people we can mention who have not numbered some religious believers among them, and some among those religious believers who have derived peace or joy from their belief.

The difficulty about greater sources of satisfaction can at least be partially answered by looking at people who have turned to the happiness to be found in religious belief from almost every other form of satisfaction and declared the happiness of religious belief greater.

Is there corresponding evidence on the other side? Can we point out persons whose *lack* of religious belief has been a source of deep satisfaction to them, who have derived serenity or joy from atheism or agnosticism? For the most part, I think, the claim is not even made. Atheists and agnostics have claimed to find freedom from fear or from restriction by abandoning religion, but they have seldom claimed that their lack of belief in itself brings them joy or serenity. The Greek Sceptics, indeed, claimed that suspending belief on all questions led to tranquility of a sort; but most sceptics have claimed at most "the tranquility of settled despair".

Of course, no matter what the consolations of religion, they must be rejected if there is no good reason to accept religious belief. But if there are good reasons, then the happiness of religious belief may be an additional piece of evidence.

Finally, it is worth noting that to try to adopt a certain view *because* that view is consoling would be the height of folly. A view adopted for other reasons may be enjoyable as well as true. Our delight may even be further proof of its truth. We sometimes find, to our delight, that we really are good at something, for example, be it mathematics or marbles, and our enjoyment may help show this. But to try to believe that we were good at mathematics or marbles just to *make* ourselves feel happy would be to court insanity.

10

The World with God in It

Let us now pause and look at the difference that necessarily exists between a theistic world view and any alternative view. It is sometimes said that religion makes no difference to our view of the universe, and some theists seem to have a view of the universe not very different from that of nontheists. But theism *should* in reason make an enormous difference in our view of the world. Let us see what this difference is, or reasonably ought to be.

First, since the theist believes the universe was created by a God whose mind is in some respects like his own, he can reasonably expect the universe to be ultimately understandable—not necessarily simple, not necessarily immediately or easily understandable, but ultimately and basically understandable. The nontheist, if he holds a chance theory, can have no assurance of this kind at all, and the nontheist who holds the natural necessity theory must realize that natural necessity may have produced in his mind a view as false as any he rejects. Thus theism gives a confidence in the understandability of the world that no other view can hold.

It might be objected that the intelligibility of the world is simply a brute fact, having no explanation. The world has

shown itself to be intelligible in the past, and this is sufficient evidence that it will continue to be so. For its being so,
no further explanation is possible.

One difficulty with this is that our confidence that the
past is a reliable guide to the future is a part of our confidence in the intelligibility of the world. If the world is not
intelligible, there is no reason why the future *should* be like
the past. But the deeper difficulty is that there seems no
reason to accept the intelligibility of the universe as a brute
fact. We know what an explanation of this intelligibility
would be like; we know of one satisfactory explanation.
Our only possible reason for refusing to explain the intelligibility of the universe is that we might not like the explanation. Imagine this transferred to a case of a more ordinary
kind: "No, we must regard this murder as brute fact, with
no explanation. Yes, I know there is an explanation that
would account for the crime, but this explanation makes
me guilty of the crime. So we must refuse to explain the
murder." Such a refusal would be obviously unreasonable
in this case, and I think it is just as obviously unreasonable
in the case of the intelligibility of the universe.

In the same way, the theist believes that the moral law is
based on the nature of God and on the nature of the universe he has made. Therefore, if the theist judges that a war
or a society is immoral, that a man or a movement is morally good, he has a right to think his judgments have a real
validity. The relativist can be expressing only his own opinions or preferences. He can, of course, say that these are the
opinions or preferences of all decent or moral people, but
on the relativist view, to call some people "decent" or "moral"
is simply to express a subjective feeling or opinion. The holder
of the absolute moral law theory can appeal to the objectivity of the moral law, but in what sense is the moral law

absolute? Experience shows that men can and do ignore the moral law. Even if conscience bothers some of these, perhaps better tranquilizers are the answer. The problem of an impersonal moral law that is part of an impersonal universe is that obligations can be felt only by a person.

The person who feels the force of the moral law without acknowledging its Source is in a better position than the relativist, but his refusal to base the moral law on anything outside of itself leaves him in a position not unlike that of the person who refuses to explain the intelligibility of the universe. The basic truths of logic and mathematics may be self-evident; they may need no proof outside themselves. But the question of why the universe is such that reason applies to it at all is still a sensible one, and one we cannot decline. Similarly, even if the basic truths of morality are somehow self-evident, we cannot evade the question of why the universe is such that a moral law exists.

We could, of course, try to think of the moral law as a necessary being. But it is not clear that the moral law is a being at all in that sense. Also, a necessary being exists whether or not anything else exists. But what would it mean to say that a moral law existed if no moral agents existed? The theist can make sense of the idea, since for him the moral law is based on the nature of God, who is a necessary Being; and thus whether or not God chooses to create other moral agents, there always exists that in his nature which would make it the case that if he created other moral agents, certain laws would be binding upon them.

The absolute moral law theorist may try to identify the moral law with something in the minds of moral agents. But if he holds the chance or natural necessity view, what confidence can he have that this is not random programming of his mind by the mindless, purposeless universe he believes in?

Thus it seems that in logic the theist and no one else should see the universe as making sense in terms of reason and in terms of morality. Furthermore, only the theist has some reason to expect that the longings for and intimations of happiness that our experience gives us are not ultimately to be frustrated. This has the consequence that only the theist can take happiness reasonably. He is under no compulsion to grab as much of it as he can, like the Epicurean, since if God is just and the universe makes moral sense, he can expect those longings for happiness to be adequately fulfilled at last "full measure, pressed down and brimming over". He does not need to fear involvement and force himself to set his happiness only on things within his control, like the Stoic, for the same reason. Of course, life as we know it can break our hearts if we expect perfect happiness from *it*. But if we treat the happiness we now receive as sustenance on the way and a promise to be fulfilled, we need neither grab for happiness nor shrink from it.

Without this hope of eventual happiness, there is a curious anomaly in the moral law itself. The moral law requires justice, but plainly life as we experience it is in many ways unjust. So if the universe is not created by a just God, who will eventually reward and punish according to justice, then the moral law that requires justice is somehow a part of an unjust universe.

Some Stoics, it is true, believed in a just God and an objective moral law but not in an afterlife. But Stoicism was an aristocratic moral theory that said in effect that we could have happiness by limiting our desires to those things within our control, and if anyone failed to do so, so much the worse for him. Stoicism is a noble creed, but it has no very hopeful message for the weak, or perhaps for most ordinary men.

Thus, in the upshot, a universe without God is also a universe without meaning, a universe in which reason is not to be trusted, the moral law has no force, and the hope of happiness is doomed to frustration. If we were forced to accept such a universe, we would have to make the best of it we could, as the Epicureans, and the Sceptics, too, in their own way, tried to do. But what can force us to such a view? No external compulsion, for too many men of all kinds reject the view. Not reason, for the view denies its validity. Not morality, for the view denies any force to morality. Not hope of happiness, for the view rejects this hope. Thus there can be *no* reasons for accepting the view that the universe is meaningless, and there are excellent reasons for accepting the theistic view, which makes sense of the intelligibility of the universe, the felt force of the moral law, and our intimations of happiness. The difficulties of accepting and understanding the theistic view may be formidable, but the difficulties of rejecting it are insurmountable. To this conclusion reason leads us, and we can reject it only by rejecting reason.

Beyond reason stands revelation, and in the final section of the book, we will see what its credentials are before the court of reason and what reason can do to explore its claims. But before we come to revelation, we can draw a few final conclusions about the view of the world that a purely rational theism can give us.

First, the theistic view gives us plentiful grounds for humility. Our reason, our morality, our hope of happiness come to us from a Person immeasurably greater than ourselves. We are creatures, and we have a Creator. This should give us grounds for thankfulness but should also give grounds for awe in the face of the greatness of creation. The message of the book of Job is that the wonder of God's creation should still our complaints. It is not just that God is powerful: any tyrant can bully us by his power, but this will not silence a Job. It is the wisdom revealed in the works of God that makes us realize we know as little of God's plans for us as we know of how to create a universe.

Our attitude toward our fellow creatures, too, should be affected. We did not create the beauty of nature, and though we have the power to destroy it, we may not have the right. Our fellow human beings receive their life at God's hands as we do, and we have no obvious rights over them. Everything belongs to God by right of creation, and for our dealings with things we may be called to account by their Owner. Our own lives, too, are not our own, and the Stoic readiness to step out of life by suicide if life became too hard is a dubious venture for a theist, as some Stoics saw.

The theist's attitude toward pains and pleasures should be affected by his conviction that the universe makes sense. If I suffer, there is a reason for it; if I have joy, there is Someone to thank for it. On the other hand, for the nontheist, pains and pleasures are equally meaningless incidents, just as no life is of any importance and no destruction is prohibited.

With regard to the moral law, the theist will have a conviction that the moral law is founded in the deepest nature of reality, that the same Power that brought him into existence and in whose reason he shares is the Power that also stands behind the moral law. The theist will recognize duties specifically to God, such as the duty of worship and the duty of obeying any commands of God even though the things commanded are not otherwise obligatory. Aside from these special obligations, which of course are unrecognized by the nontheist, it is less clear that the theist and the holder of an absolute moral law position will differ on obligations.

Some form of the Golden Rule, which includes both the notion of justice and that of benevolence, could be recognized as the basis of morality by both the theist and the holder of the absolute moral law theory. Both presumably would recognize special obligations to parents and children, and special obligations with regard to husbands and wives. Both could recognize special obligations with regard to truth, the evils of greed and lust, and so on. The "second table" of the ten commandments, which has to do with duties to man, and the commandment to love our neighbor as ourselves can be recognized by the nontheist as well as by the theist.

The theist is most likely to disagree with the nontheist on specific obligations that go beyond a certain minimum. Murder is an obvious evil, while certain forms of domination and exploitation are far from obviously evil. If man is made only for himself and for present pleasures and enjoyments, kinds of behavior toward other people that cause them no unhappiness and no obvious loss may seem permissible. If man's decisions have only a temporal effect, we will regard them differently than if they contribute to a personality that will exist for eternity.

It is true that the believer in an afterlife *may* tend to show less urgent concern for suffering and injustice here on earth than those who believe that this life is the sum total of man's existence. But the very urgency of those who believe that this life is the last chance may lead them to increase the sufferings of the world in a hope for some drastic solution to human ills. Far more often, though, the magnitude of human misery and the difficulties of alleviating it can cause despair. The theist, precisely because he believes good will triumph in the end, can attack the problems of the world without either frenzy or despair.

Still, without revelation, the ethics of the purely rational theist may not be markedly different from those of the conscientious upholder of the absolute moral law view. It is about the foundation of the moral law and the ultimate purpose of morality that the theist will disagree with the nontheist. Both can agree that selfishness and hate damage the human person, but they will disagree on the value and durability of what is being damaged. Theism should, then, have a profound effect on the mental world of the theist and thereby on his actions. This will be minimized by laziness, cowardice, and other vices on the part of the theist. A given theist may be a worse person in many respects than a given nontheist. It is to be expected that theism should improve whatever character the theist has, just as training should improve whatever athletic abilities a man has. But people do not start out on a level in character any more than in athletic ability. An untrained "natural athlete" may hit a tennis ball better than I, but training has improved my abilities and would improve his.

All this presumes that the person in question acts as his belief would reasonably seem to indicate he should act. A man may, of course, admit in theory that God exists and makes certain moral demands but do nothing about it, just as a man may admit in theory that cigarette smoking injures his health and will eventually kill him but continue to smoke. But there is a great deal of strain in behavior of this kind; we are more likely to try to make our beliefs fit our actions than to face an inconsistency between belief and action.

Paradoxically, perhaps the best way of evading theism is to ostensibly embrace it. A tame god—a god who shares our own prejudices or panders to our timidity or guarantees us happiness in exchange for keeping some neat and unburdensome set of rules—is a great defense against the real God and his absolute demands. And an ostensible atheism that rejects the attempt of a family or society to impose a false god who is an idol or a good luck charm or a demon can be the first step toward the true God, who keeps to no rule books, who accepts no limited commitments, whose demands are as tremendous as his promises.

PART III

REVELATION

11

The Credentials of Revelation

Reason, basing itself on experience, can take us a certain way in understanding the nature of the universe and our place in it. But if reason is correct in telling us that a Creator and Ruler of the universe exists, then there is at least a possibility that this Person may have in some way or at some time revealed himself to man—told us about himself and made it clear that the revelation does indeed come from him. If he has done so, then the content of the revelation must be understandable by human reason, but its truth or falsity will not be directly decidable by reason. If God indeed tells us something, then reason will tell us to believe what he has told us, *because* he has told us. Similarly, we accept on authority the statements of experts in various fields, once we are convinced they are experts. But reason must, of course, judge the credentials of any alleged revelation. If reason tells us a certain statement is a revelation from God, it follows that we ought to believe it. But if reason gives us no reason to suppose a given statement is a revelation from God, then we cannot believe it on those grounds. (Although, of course, we may believe it on other grounds; "It needs no ghost risen from the grave" to tell us that every villain in Denmark is a knave.)

Thus, if anyone holds, as traditional Christianity does, that God has given a revelation to man, it is up to reason to test whether or not the alleged revelation is in fact a revelation from God.

How can reason do this? It may be helpful to begin by considering a case that is parallel in some ways. Suppose we are reading a fascinating but puzzling story that is being serialized in a periodical. Someone claiming to be its author offers to explain the story to us. One thing that would help convince us that the claim was true would be the ability of the alleged author to explain the story so far in a way that clears up our main puzzles and confusions about it. Another would be his ability to predict what would happen in future installments of the story. But the most convincing proof that could be offered would be an ability to control the course of events in the story. If the alleged author says, "Look here: to prove I am the author, I'll put in the next installment a taxi driver with your name", and such a character does indeed appear in the next installment, then this shows at the least that the alleged author can influence the real author (if we rule out as a fantastic coincidence that the next installment just happened to have a taxi driver with our name).

Now, something very much like these three conditions is the traditional credentials of revelation. The ordinary Christian, at the time of Christ, and now, has found that the teaching of Christ makes sense of life as he experiences it, that the life of Christ makes sense of the whole tendency of the Old Testament (as well as of many specific hints and statements in the Old Testament), and finally that certain things done by Christ can be explained only on the hypothesis that Christ controlled, or was able to influence him who controls, life and death, matter and energy.

Let us consider these points in reverse order. We saw in chapter 3 that alleged "scientific" or philosophical objections to the possibility of miracles could not be sustained. Thus if our documents allege that Christ rose from the dead, that he changed water to wine, multiplied loaves and fishes, stilled the storm, raised Lazarus, and so on, we cannot rule out these claims a priori. Whether or not our historical evidence warrants our believing that these events actually occurred is another and more complex question. We have several choices:

(a) We may claim that the alleged events are complete fabrications.
(b) We may admit that something like the alleged events occurred but try to explain them naturalistically.
(c) We may admit that the events occurred, explain them as divine interventions, and take them as guaranteeing whatever statements or claims Christ made.

In eliminating (a) and (b), we need to consider expert testimony but not necessarily to be experts ourselves. Indeed, the situation is not unlike that of a case at law where, since issues of great importance are at stake, we allow ordinary men and women to reach the best conclusions they can in light of expert testimony. There is no lack of experts on both sides of the question, and many sensible and hard-headed men and women have come to the conclusion that fabrication can be ruled out, that naturalistic explanations fail, and that miracle is the only reasonable explanation. But only God can work miracles, and he would not work them in support of false claims.

In the matter of what claims were in fact made, there are allegations that certain claims were added to the documents later by the community of believers. Again, the plausibility of this must be examined in the light of experience. Consider, for example, Christ's claim to forgive sins on his own authority. If Sue has injured Sally, and Sam claims to forgive Sue, the claim is nonsensical: Sam is not the injured party. Only God, who is the Source of the moral law, can reasonably make such a claim. And to remove this claim from the Gospel account is impossible without making a shambles of the whole account. Christ "went about doing good", says Peter (Acts 10:38); but if we remove miraculous healings and forgiveness of sins from the account, very little is left. And the old dilemma still holds: if Christ claimed to be God, he was speaking the truth, or was lying, or was insane. If common sense and available evidence rule out the last two hypotheses, the first must be true. And if Christ is not God, come to heal and forgive, even his death becomes nothing but a regrettable interruption in the teaching work of a rabbi who taught little more than a deeper understanding of the traditional Jewish doctrines.

Thus hundreds of thousands of intelligent and sensible Christians have come to the conclusion that only the traditional understanding of Christ, as the Son of God come to redeem mankind, makes sense of the historical and documentary evidence as we have it. Similarly, they have come to the conclusion that the historical and documentary evidence about the Jewish people can best be explained as a preparation for that mission. Each particular prophecy or hint or indication can perhaps be explained as meaning something different, but the whole body of the tradition seems to point to only one reasonable conclusion. "If the Messiah should come," they challenge their Jewish brethren, "what more could he do than Jesus did?" And in response to this challenge, Orthodox Judaism has emphasized the apocalyptic aspects of the prophecies, so that the Orthodox Jew expects of the coming of the Messiah what the Christian expects of the Second Coming of Christ. Liberal Judaism has allegorized and explained away the prophecies, changing essentially the character of historical Judaism.

In both these cases, we have given a mere hint or sketch of the line of argument that convinces Christians of the authenticity of Christ's message. With regard to the way in which this message makes sense of life as it is experienced, we can say a little more, for this depends less on examination of history and of documents.

The first area of experience that seems to be illuminated by the Christian message is the area of sin and guilt. As we pointed out earlier, part of our perception of the moral law is our realization that we ourselves have failed to measure up to that law. Despite widespread efforts to explain away guilt, it seems to be a universal experience; and efforts to suppress guilt feelings in one area—sexual behavior, for instance—seem to lead to increased guilt feelings in other areas—for example, in the area of war or racism. Christianity holds that guilt is genuine but that our repentance will be met by God's mercy. No theory that denies the reality of guilt can satisfy us in light of our experience, but any theory that admits the reality of guilt but offers no hope for its forgiveness would lead to despair. Forgiveness without repentance would be merely glossing over or ignoring guilt, which would ease our fears but not satisfy our moral sense. Repentance therefore is a necessity, but the more we need to repent, the less we are able. The Christian belief that God has become man and died for our sins solves this dilemma.

At first the idea of vicarious atonement—of a sinless Christ dying for our sins—seems puzzling or even repellent. But as we reflect on it, our understanding grows. From our own point of view, we realize our guilt and helplessness to make any adequate reparation. For God merely to dismiss our sins, to let us off without punishment despite our guilt, might be a relief from our fears, but would it be morally satisfying? If sin is a serious matter, if God has promised retribution, can we expect God to say in effect, "I've changed my mind; I won't punish you after all"? But when we see that someone else, someone entirely without guilt of his own, has taken our place, has undergone our deserved punishment, this can give us a whole new attitude. Our motives for repentance are at once greater and less self-interested. No longer fear of punishment but gratitude and shame and sympathy impel us to repent. When this person who suffers for our sins is not just another human person but a Person who is God, new depth and dimension are added.

Our whole attitude toward Christ, the God-Man, becomes different. What external help, what healings, what nourishing, what blessing could give us the attitude Christians have toward Christ? Only *costly* love, only self-sacrifice can show perfect love. And since God cannot in his own nature suffer, he must become man. Once we grasp the idea of an incarnate God suffering for our sins, any other solution to the problem of sin can be seen to be inadequate.

If we think of God as somehow apart from Christ and demanding punishment, even of the innocent, to satisfy some sort of vengeance, we get a caricature of the idea of atonement that quite rightly repels unbelievers. But Christians believe that the Person who demands the sacrifice is one with the Person who suffers. There is only one remedy for our condition, and it is God himself who bears the cost of that remedy.

Once we realize this, we begin to see that self-sacrificing love, the love that suffers so that another may not suffer, is the deepest kind of human love. If God's love was less than this, human love would, impossibly, be greater than God's love. We begin to realize that sacrifice offered and accepted is the form that love must take in a fallen world and that God must be our leader and exemplar in this as in everything else. As C. S. Lewis points out:

What do we mean when we talk of God helping us? We mean God putting into us a bit of Himself, so to speak. He lends us a little of His reasoning powers and that is how we think: He puts a little of His love into us and that is how we love one another.... But unfortunately we now need God's help in order to do something which God, in His own nature, never does at all—to surrender, to suffer, to submit, to die. Nothing in God's nature corresponds to this process at all. So that the one road for which we now need God's leadership most of all is a road God, in His own nature, has never walked. God can share only what He has: this thing, in His own nature, He has not.

But supposing God became a man—suppose our human nature which can suffer and die was amalgamated with God's nature in one person—then that person could help us. He could surrender His will, and suffer and die, because He was man; and He could do it perfectly because He was God. You and I can go through this process only if God does it in us; but God can do it only if He becomes man. Our attempts at this dying will succeed only if we men share in God's dying, just as our thinking can succeed only because it is a drop out of the ocean of His intelligence: but we cannot share God's dying unless God dies; and He cannot die except by being a man. That is the sense in which He pays our debt, and suffers for us what He Himself need not suffer at all.[1]

[1] *Mere Christianity* (San Francisco: Harper, 2001), pp. 57–58.

As we have already said, also, the Christian doctrine of the Fall of man corresponds with our perception of a terrible gap between mankind's ideals and performance. So in this whole area of sin and guilt, Christianity seems to fit in with our experience.

Another area in which Christianity seems to ring true is in the area of an adequate direction and purpose to life. The feeling of "Is that all there is?" is inescapable in even the most satisfactory human life, and the mere extension of our experience beyond life would simply give us an eternity of our own inadequacies. But on the Christian view, man is made to know and enjoy God for all eternity. Since God is infinite, there will always be more to know; since God is the Source of all joy and delight, there will always be more to enjoy. Faced with the good things of this life in which good and bad are mixed, we can choose the element of good in an evil state of affairs and concentrate on the bad in a good state of affairs and thus choose treachery, cruelty, dishonesty for the sake of goods they will bring us.

But faced with the pure and infinite goodness of God, we will be utterly content, utterly absorbed in enjoyment, always doing what we prefer because nothing could be preferable to this. Christianity thus offers us a really adequate notion of perfect happiness. In this happiness, says Christianity, we shall delightedly share our own vision of God, a unique vision we were made to appreciate and share. This sharing of the vision of God, metaphorically expressed in the vision of the heavenly choir that cries, "Holy, Holy, Holy", will be the full embodiment of the sharing of vision dimly hinted at by philosophy, by art and literature, by teaching at its best.

Given that the perfect Good, once experienced, is totally overwhelming, we can see that the only possibility of a really free choice of God is a situation where the full glory is veiled and we must endure, suffer, and overcome to choose the Good. Thus the basic reason for suffering can be seen in a new perspective when we realize that we can enjoy the Glory as ones who have *freely* chosen God only if life exhibits the pain and difficulty, the ambiguity and tests of faith that it in fact exhibits. Thus Christianity, properly understood, views life as intelligible and as infinitely worthwhile because life as it is can be seen as a necessary means to an infinitely desirable goal.

Again, Lewis has expressed it in a way upon which it is hard to improve:

> I am considering not how, but why, He makes each soul unique. If He had no use for all these differences, I do not know why He should have created more souls than one.... Why else were individuals created, but that God, loving all infinitely, should love each differently? And this difference, so far from impairing, floods with meaning the love of all blessed. If all experienced God in the same way and returned Him an identical worship, the song of the Church triumphant would have no symphony, it would be like an orchestra in which all the instruments played the same note.... Heaven is a city, and a Body, because the blessed remain eternally different: a society, because each has something to tell all the others—fresh and ever fresh news of the "My God" whom each finds in Him whom all praise as "Our God". For doubtless the continually successful, yet never completed, attempt by each soul to communicate its unique vision to all others (and that by means whereof earthly art and philosophy are but clumsy imitations) is also among the ends for which the individual was created.[2]

---

[2] *The Problem of Pain* (San Francisco: Harper, 2001), pp. 154–56.

Finally, Christianity can give us an insight into our experience of other people. "What a piece of work is man", and humanity at its best is glorious. But how seldom humanity is at its best. The naïve exaltation of man by the humanist who believes that man can be perfected by social engineering or by psychiatric or behavioralistic reconstruction of his psyche is as far from the mark as the disregard of human potentialities by the cynic. Man is both better and worse than any view except the Christian view can adequately express. On the Christian view, even the dullest and most limited of us can grow in God into a glorious being beyond our present dreams of divinity. Even the noblest of us now can take the path that will lead him eventually away from God to nothingness. And this can and must affect our attitude to our fellow humans. To quote Lewis again:

> It is a serious thing to live in a society of possible gods and goddesses, to remember that the dullest and most uninteresting person you talk to may one day be a creature which, if you saw it now, you would be strongly tempted to worship, or else a horror and a corruption such as you now meet, if at all, only in a nightmare. All day long we are, in some degree, helping each other to one or other of these destinations. It is in the light of these overwhelming possibilities, it is with the awe and the circumspection proper to them, that we should conduct all our dealings with one another, all friendships, all loves, all play, all politics. There are no *ordinary* people. You have never talked to a mere mortal. Nations, cultures, arts, civilization—these are mortal, and their life is to ours as the life of a gnat. But it is immortals whom we joke with, work with, marry, snub, and exploit—immortal horrors or everlasting splendours. This does not mean that we are to be perpetually solemn. We must play. But our merriment must be of that kind (and it

is, in fact, the merriest kind) which exists between people who have, from the outset, taken each other seriously—no flippancy, no superiority, no presumption. And our charity must be a real and costly love, with deep feeling for the sins in spite of which we love the sinner—no mere tolerance or indulgence which parodies love as flippancy parodies merriment. Next to the Blessed Sacrament itself, your neighbour is the holiest object presented to your senses. If he is your Christian neighbour he is holy in almost the same way, for in him also Christ *vere latitat*—the glorifier and the glorified, Glory Himself, is truly hidden.[3]

[3] *The Weight of Glory* (San Francisco: Harper, 2001), pp. 45–46.

12

God

Even if we accept the credentials of the Christian revelation, many of the things revealed are puzzling. Theology is the continual attempt to do what we can to understand the great mysteries of religion. The "mysteries" of religion, of course, are neither mere puzzles with some simple solution nor completely incomprehensible. We understand something about them but can continually increase our understanding of them. This increased understanding will never contradict our earlier understanding but may put it in an entirely new perspective. The process grows less puzzling when we realize that this is exactly what happens in the case of our knowledge of other human beings. We never completely understand even those we are closest to, but we can continually understand them better than we did, so long as we keep trying. When we stop with a partial understanding of a human person and treat that partial understanding as if it were complete, we have the analogue in human relations to something that can happen in theology—the attempt to treat God's revelation as something that can be completely contained in our formulations.

But throwing up our hands and making no effort to understand God's revelation, treating it as incomprehensible, also has its analogues in human relations. The refusal to try to understand (because "women are incomprehensible" or because "men are impossible") can be as damaging in human relationships as obscurantism is in theology. Continual attempts at deeper understanding and constant humility about the success of our efforts is no bad formula in either theology or human relations.

In the remaining chapters of this book, we will attempt to increase our understanding of certain key points in the Christian revelation. We will do this partly because lack of understanding or partial understanding of such points can be a stumbling block to those outside of Christianity, and in this respect our discussion will return to the concerns of the first part of this book: answering objections to faith. But we will also be interested in increased understanding of these things because they can provide a positive motive for belief. In a few cases, to know a human being better is to dislike him more: "Only those who really know X can detest him as he deserves." But in most cases, the proverbs are right; to understand all is to forgive all, to know better is to love better. And once the light is removed from under the bushel of misunderstandings, it can illuminate far more, giving us more cause to believe Christianity because it makes sense of everything else.

Probably the greatest source of misunderstandings is the idea of God himself. There are minor difficulties over his omnipotence, which of course does not imply the power to do what is self-contradictory in itself, like making a square circle, or self-contradictory when joined with the idea of being done by God, like making a world not made by God or making a stone that cannot be lifted. But more important difficulties arise when we consider God's knowledge.

Christians have traditionally believed that God knows all things and that "all things" includes all future things. This belief, combined with an idea of the unchangeability of God, based partly on revelation and partly on theological speculation, creates a number of difficulties about God and time. If God cannot change, it is said, then his knowledge cannot change; and if his knowledge concerns (among other things) the world, how can the world change? And even if we avoid this difficulty, there is another. If God knows yesterday what I will do today, how can I have my freedom? If an event is not already settled and inevitable, how can it be known in advance, and if it is known in advance, how can it not be settled and inevitable? There are several ways out of these problems.

1. We can accept the apparent consequences of fore-knowledge and deny free will; this is the path that the early Calvinists and other Christian predestinarians sometimes seem to have followed, though some contemporary Calvinists would challenge this interpretation.

2. We can defend free will by denying foreknowledge, which seems to run counter to the unchangeableness and omniscience of God.

3. We can attempt to reconcile unchangeability and fore-knowledge with free will, as many of the greatest Christian thinkers have believed they could do.

If the third alternative were impossible, there would be no doubt that the second alternative would have to be embraced by the Christian. For, as we saw in chapter 4, any determinist view makes God the only moral agent, and this makes nonsense of Christianity's call to repentance and prom-ise of forgiveness. I think myself that the third alternative *is* possible, but I also think that the second alternative is less alarming than it seems. Let us explore it before going on to consider the third alternative.

First, if we are to understand change, we must distinguish between relational and nonrelational properties. The relational properties of a thing may change without any change in the thing itself. If I walk around a square white stone that weighs one hundred pounds, the relation of the stone to *me* constantly changes, but the stone remains square and white, and its weight does not change. Even if God were totally unchangeable in all his nonrelational properties, some of his relational properties *must* change if there is genuine change in the world. If I come near to God, then God is nearer to me. If I go farther from God, then God is farther from me. Plainly, knowledge is a relational property; and once we see that some of God's relational properties *must* change because the things that are related to him change, then it becomes easier to entertain the idea that his knowledge changes because the objects of his knowledge change.

The difficulty about omniscience may be answerable in this way: if the world is genuinely changing, then we may wish to say that some propositions about the future are not *now* true or false but will *become* true or false depending on what happens. If God's omniscience means that he knows all true propositions, then it may be no restriction on that omniscience not to know propositions that are not now either true or false. In allowing man free will, God abdicates some of his power—he allows certain things to depend genuinely on our choice. It would not be astounding if he also abdicated some of his knowledge in giving man free will. In fact, if knowledge is really incompatible with free will, and free will is required by the Christian revelation, this is just what the Christian *must* say. And if the actions of a free being are unknowable in principle, then it is no more a limitation on God's knowledge not to know the logically unknowable than it is a limitation on God's power not to be able to do the logically undoable.

Does this mean that God knows no more of the future than we do? No, for just as a master chessplayer playing a complete novice can bring the game to whatever outcome he likes at any time he likes, God can foresee all possible choices that a finite creature can make and bring about certain results whatever choice is made. Nor does this make a mockery of freedom, for man is judged on the choices he makes, not on whether he achieves his purposes.

This picture does, however, involve a genuine uncertainty on the part of God about the choices that will be made and thus about the judgment deserved by the individual. On this view, God may not know when he creates a person, or now, whether that person will be saved or lost. This does seem incompatible with some parts of the Christian revelation.

For this reason as well as for others, it may be well to explore the third alternative, that foreknowledge is compatible with free will. We must start by discussing spirits and their relation to space, which will help us understand God's relation to time. On the traditional view, God is a spirit, and a spirit is a particular individual entity that neither occupies space nor has weight nor is directly knowable by our senses. Nonmaterialists in all ages have thought that our own minds are an example of a particular individual reality of this kind, and materialists (from the philosophers whom Plato compared to the Titans who tried to pull down Heaven, up to modern behaviorists) have denied the existence of any particular individual reality of this kind, either a nonmaterial soul for man or a nonmaterial God. We will say more of this dispute in the final chapter of this book.

For the moment, assume for the sake of argument that spirits exist and that some, unlike the human soul, are "pure" spirits, not embodied. What is the relation of a pure spirit to space? It is not *in* space; therefore it cannot have parts the way material things can. Knowledge and will are not "parts" of the soul as arms and legs are parts of the body. A pure spirit cannot be *in* a place in the usual sense; it cannot be surrounded by other matter as a body can (nor can it be so many feet from a fixed point, etc.). But we can say that it is "at", in a certain sense, whatever point in space it is acting. Even an embodied soul like ours is not *in* our brain or body as water is in a cup but is locatable where our brain or body is only because it acts on them.

God, then, is not *in* any spatial location, but since he is acting on all things, to keep them in existence, he is "at" every point in space. This is what is meant by the "omnipresence" of God. Being a pure spirit, he has no parts; it is not the case that part of him is here, part there; *all* of him is at all places. Thus the old paradoxical statement that "God is a circle whose circumference is nowhere and whose center is everywhere." God is not contained in the universe or in any part of it ("whose circumference is nowhere") and is totally present at any point in space ("whose center is everywhere"). We cannot say that God is in the universe; indeed, considering that he sustains every part of the universe in existence and every part of the universe is open to him, we might just as well say that the universe is "in" God.

C. S. Lewis puts this doctrine poetically when he has his
angelic beings in *Perelandra* sing: "He dwells (all of Him
dwells) within the seed of the smallest flower and is not
cramped: Deep Heaven [space] is inside Him who is inside
the seed and does not distend Him. Blessed be He! ... He
is in every place. Not some of Him in one place and some
of Him in another, but in each place the whole [God] even
in the smallness beyond thought." [1]

Now, it is quite possible to deny that this idea of the
relation of God to space is *true*, but it seems to me that it is
quite *clear*. And unless the behaviorist or materialist view is
correct, we ourselves are spirits and have direct acquain-
tance with one concrete individual, our own mind, that is
nonspatial.

When we come to the relation of God to time, however,
we are on more debatable ground. It is plain from the Old
and New Testaments that God always exists, that "he is from
everlasting to everlasting." Thus just as no stretch of space
contains God, no stretch of time contains him. However, if
we are to continue the parallel with space, we must say that
God has no temporal parts any more than he has spatial
parts and that all of him is present at every point in time.
Just as we said that God is not *in* space, we might say that
God is not *in* time.

What would it mean to say this? One obvious thing that
would be meant is that God does not change his nonrelational properties or modify his nature with time, as human
beings do. My sense of smell may have been better when I
was young; my temper may be better when I am old. Nothing parallel occurs with God, "with whom there is no alter-
ation or shadow caused by change" (James 1:17, NAB).

[1] *Perelandra* (New York: Scribner, 2001), pp. 184, 185.

But beyond the essential unity and sameness of God's nature at all times, what else is meant by the idea that God is "outside of" time, not "in" time?

One interpretation of what this would mean, which goes back at least to Boethius and which seems to solve certain difficulties raised by scriptural statements, is the idea that God does not experience events successively but grasps past, present, and future in one "eternal now". Just as all *places* are equally present to God, and God's presence at one place is not different from his presence in another place, so, it is said, all times are equally present to God, and God's presence at one time is not different from his presence at another time.

One difficulty in understanding this is that it is totally outside our experience. If the traditional idea of the soul is correct, man's mind is nonspatial and thus can understand the nonspatial aspect of God. Man's mind is also nontemporal in the sense that it is not bound to the continual change of the material universe. Many ticks of the clock can seem short to him, or a few ticks can seem long. And it is not only seeming. A man can think twenty thoughts in a few seconds or hold one thought for hours. He is not bound to the time scale of material objects. The medievals expressed this by saying that the "duration" of material things was time, the "duration" of man was aeviternity or sempiternity ("almost" eternity), and the "duration" of God was the "eternal now" of eternity.

We can, of course, think of past or future events, some of which were or will be before others and others of which were or will be after others, all together at one time. The idea of eternity as an "eternal now" says that God can see events that to our perception *have* happened, *are* happening, or *will* happen all together in this fashion, knowing their temporal relations but not experiencing them successively.

A spatial analogy helps some people make sense of this notion. Consider a one-dimensional creature, x, living on a line and able to progress along the line in only one direction:

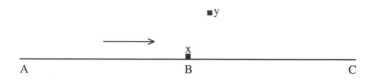

All points on portion AB of the line are "past" to x, and all points on portion BC are "future". He can make no sense of experiencing the whole line AC without experiencing its points successively. But the two-dimensional creature y above the line can perceive all points on the line without experiencing them successively. The difficulty with this analogy is that the portion of the line BC (the "future") is imagined as "already there" in some sense to be perceived by y. But if the real future is "already there" in some sense, we seem to be back to determinism, with its attendant difficulties. It is not the dimensional analogy that is at fault; this may contain a valuable clue. The difficulty is that we cannot imagine the future as known if it does not exist, and we cannot imagine it as existing if it is not somehow fixed and therefore inevitable and unalterable.

It has been pointed out that knowing something is different from making it happen and therefore that God's knowing that I make a choice does not mean God's making me make that choice. This is true enough, but the problem is that we cannot imagine knowing something unless *something* has made it happen. And if God knew before I was born what I would do today, how could it have been *me* making it happen, since I was not yet born?

The difficulty, however, may be in our own limitations. We could create a similar pseudoproblem by saying, "If God is present to me here and now, and if he is also causing some event in another galaxy now, then something present here can instantaneously affect something in another galaxy." As we can see from what has been said, God is no more *here* now than he is in any other place he is acting. He is in no place; he acts at all places. In a parallel fashion, we create a pseudoproblem by saying, "If God knew *yesterday* what I would do today ..." For God is no more located at any time than he is located at any place. The only sense in which he acts in New York is that his actions affect New York. The only sense in which he knows *yesterday* is that certain objects of his knowledge are yesterday's events. God's knowing does not occur yesterday, or today, or tomorrow; it occurs outside of time altogether. God's power is exercised outside of space, but we can experience its effects only in space. God's knowledge is *of* things in time, but his knowing does not occur at any point of time.

It may be that those who believe they understand this notion are mistaken and that we can really make no sense of nontemporal knowing. If so, there may be some other solution to the apparent dilemma that foreknowledge creates. But if we are genuinely faced with a choice between certain kinds of foreknowledge in God and freedom in man, then Christianity leaves us no choice but to opt for freedom over foreknowledge.

13

The Son of God

Traditional Christianity makes two puzzling statements that involve the Son of God:

1. There are three Persons "in" God—Father, Son, and Holy Spirit—but only one God.
2. The Son of God, who is God, was also "incarnated" or "made flesh" in Jesus Christ, who is truly man.

To understand these statements better, we must think about persons and their natures, for the traditional way of explaining the two statements above is as follows:

1. There are three Persons in God, but only one divine nature.
2. There is only one Person who is both the Son and the man Jesus, but he has two natures, human and divine.

We can begin to understand what is meant by *nature* here by considering the essential components of any rational nature. By *nature*, we mean a power or ability to act. A rational nature must have the power to *know* and the power to *will*. These are separable in thought but not in reality, since will without knowledge would not be will but mere blind impulse; and knowledge without attention, which is the will to attend to what is presented to us, would not be knowledge but merely sensation imposed on us.

Part of what we mean by saying that Father, Son, and Holy Spirit have one nature is that none of the three could will anything that the others did not also will, and none of the three could know anything that the others did not know. Part of what we mean by saying that Christ had a human nature as well as a divine nature is that he had a human will that was distinct from the divine will shared by the Persons of the Trinity and that he had human knowledge that was distinct from the divine knowledge shared by the Persons of the Trinity. As God, Christ could say to the storm, "Be still", and it was still. As man, Christ could say to the Father, "Father, if thou art willing, remove this cup from me; nevertheless not my will, but thine, be done" (Luke 22:42).

The meaning of *person* is more complex but also more familiar. Each of us is a person, possessing knowledge and will but not identical with our knowledge and will. I will, I know, but I am neither my will nor my knowledge. The Person who is the Second Person of the Trinity has a divine will and divine knowledge but is not the same as that will or that knowledge. The same Person has a human will and human knowledge but is not the same as that will or knowledge. The other two Persons of the Trinity share the Son's divine knowledge and divine will but not his human knowledge or human will. Something faintly like this occurs when by training we acquire a "second nature". We can say things like, "As a philosopher, Austin was pitiless to errors and to intellectual laziness, but as a father he was kind and even indulgent." The same person, Austin, has one character *as* a philosopher, another *as* a man. This is, of course, a "way of speaking", but a very natural one.

Something even more enlightening occurs when a good actor acts a part. We can say things like, "As Maurice Evans, actor and director, he knows exactly where behind the curtain Polonius is hiding. But as Hamlet, prince of Denmark, he knows nothing of Polonius' presence. It is not until he hears the noise and sees the movement that Hamlet becomes aware of the hidden figure, and when he kills he believes he has killed the king." The good actor, in other words, must maintain a sort of dual knowledge. The actor must not let the prince know that Polonius is there, or there will be no realism in the discovery of Polonius. But the actor must not let himself be submerged in the prince, or he might really kill the actor playing Polonius.

Of course, these are only pale reflections of the reality, since nothing in our experience really parallels the experience of having two natures, any more than anything parallels sharing our will and knowledge with other persons. We can imagine an artificial case: triplets presented somehow with identical experiences and so much alike that they always make the same choices. All three triplets may know the same fact in the same way, but the first triplet's awareness of the fact is not the same as the second's awareness of it. A more natural case is acting in close cooperation with someone we know deeply and work with perfectly: dancing, working, making love. Each person is aware of what the other is aware, and each is aware of the other's awareness. Each wills the same thing at the same moment.

But, of course, if Christianity is right, then the closest we come to the experience of the Persons of the Trinity in sharing knowledge and will, and to the experience of Christ in having two natures, is the experience of God's life in us. "It is no longer I who live, but Christ who lives in me", says Paul (Galatians 2:20). "If a man loves me, he will keep my word, and my Father will love him, and we will come to him and make our home with him" (John 14:23); and "I will pray the Father, and he will give you another Counselor, to be with you for ever, even the Spirit of truth ... you know him, for he dwells with you, and will be in you" (John 14:16–17). We do not know with God's knowledge, or love with God's will, but his knowledge and will are working within us. "The spirit of adoption cries within us Abba, Father" (Rom 8:16), and someday we will know as we are known, as Paul tells us (1 Cor 13:12). This may seem too audacious, but it is Christ himself who moves from "I am in the Father and the Father is in me" to the words we have just quoted (John 14 passim) and prays "that they may be one, even as we are one" (John 17:11), "that they may all be one; even as thou, Father, art in me, and I in thee, that they also may be in us" (John 17:21).

Christ's body, too, is the body of a Person who is God, so that he can say to Philip, "He who has seen me has seen the Father" (John 14:9). Since God in his own nature does not have a body, cannot be seen by eyes, if it were not for the Incarnation the request to see God in the literal sense would be meaningless. But if a Person who is God takes human nature and a human body, then I am seeing "God's body" when I see the body of the Person who is God but also man.

Of course, the death of the man Jesus, who was also the Person who is God, does not mean the "death of God". Even you and I, if Christianity is true, will be conscious after death and will retain those powers of knowledge and will that depend on the spiritual part of our nature. (We will, for example, be able to feel joy or sorrow but not hot or cold.) The Son, of course, during the three days when he was dead retained his divine knowledge and will and as much of his human knowledge and will as was consistent with the death of his body. After the Resurrection, he regained, and still retains, his former bodily powers, changed and increased in certain ways, as ours shall be at the final resurrection.

The doctrines of which we have been speaking seem incomprehensible to many but not usually repellent. The doctrine of the Atonement, on the other hand, seems morally objectionable to some. The germ of the answer to this sort of difficulty can be found in our discussion on pages 139–40, but the answer needs expansion and explanation. We must begin with the idea of the Fall of man.

The relevant parts of the traditional Christian doctrine about the Fall can be summarized as follows:

1. God created all things without exception good, and because they are good "No *nature* (i.e., no positive reality) is bad and the word *Bad* denotes merely privation of good...."

2. What we call bad things are good things perverted.... This perversion arises when a conscious creature becomes more interested in itself than in God and wishes to exist "on its own". This is the sin of Pride. The first creature who ever committed it was Satan "the proud angel who turned from God to himself, not wishing to be a subject, but to rejoice like a tyrant in having subjects of his own...."

3. From this doctrine of good and evil it follows (a) that good can exist without evil ... but not evil without good ... (b) that good and bad angels have the same Nature, happy when it adheres to God, and miserable when it adheres to itself....

4. Though God has made all creatures good He foreknows that some will voluntarily make themselves bad ... and also

foreknows the good use which He will then make of their badness. For as He shows His benevolence in *creating* good Natures, He shows His justice in *exploiting* evil wills. . . .

8. The Fall consisted of Disobedience. . . . The apple was "not bad or harmful except in so far as it was forbidden", and the only point of forbidding it was to instill obedience "which virtue in a rational creature (the emphasis is on *creature*; that which though rational is merely a creature, not self-existent being) is, as it were the mother and guardian of *all* virtues. . . ."

9. But while the fall *consisted* in Disobedience it resulted, like Satan's, from Pride. . . .

10. Since the Fall consisted in man's Disobedience to his superior, it was punished by man's loss of Authority over his inferiors: that is chiefly over his passions and his physical organism. . . . Man has called for anarchy: God lets him have it. . . .[1]

To emphasize two points not completely clear in this quotation: First, the sin of the first representatives of mankind lost man a privilege that was not his by nature: the right to happiness in Heaven by direct knowledge of, and delight in, God. Second, the Fall did not make individual descendants of our first parents guilty of any actual sin: only our own misdeeds can do that. But it did deprive all their descendants of certain helps to virtue and render them weaker and more liable to fall into actual sin.

We have remarked that there are obvious empirical reasons for thinking that man is in some sort of mess. The

[1] C. S. Lewis, *Preface to "Paradise Lost"* (Oxford: Oxford University Press, 1942), pp. 66–70. The omissions consist of quotes giving the source of these doctrines in St. Augustine and illustrations of their use by Milton. Reprinted by permission of the publisher.

distance between our aspirations and our performance calls for some sort of explanation, and popular science obliges with a dozen incompatible theories: Freud, for example, blames civilization, and some currently popular vulgarizers of anthropology blame our animal inheritance of aggressiveness. The Christian idea of an original moral failure by the first representatives of mankind is at least as plausible as any alternative and seems to offer a more accurate pointer to the root of the trouble: all our drives (not just our libido or our aggressiveness) are out of our control, and "the evil that we will not, we do."

Can God, then, merely overrule from without the mess in which our own choices have landed us? To do so would be to treat man as irresponsible, like a mischievous animal who has to be cleaned up after and retrained or restrained. Man, then, must work his way out of the difficulty. But the difficulty is precisely with man's own nature, making it impossible for him to do so. If my painting goes wrong, I can repair it with brush and scraper; if these go wrong, I can try to put them right. But if my hand and brain go wrong, I am lost.

Thus we have the apparent dilemma: How can we be helped from outside without taking away our self-respect? How can we help ourselves, since we are damaged in the very faculty we need?

Let us begin with the obvious rule gained from experience: those who can best help us in our difficulties are those who have faced and overcome similar difficulties. From the young husband or wife seeking the help of an older married couple, to AA or Synanon, the rule holds. So we begin to see why God must become man, become "like us in all things except sin", in order to help us without destroying our integrity.

The problem is that duty, however dimly seen, runs counter to inclination. God in his own nature can never experience an inclination counter to duty, for his nature is pure love and goodness. But if God becomes man, he can preach to the crowds however weary he is, love his disciples no matter how unteachable they seem ("Do you want us to bid fire come down from heaven and consume them?" ask James and John [John!], and Jesus says wearily, "You do not know what manner of spirit you are of" [Lk 19:54]). He can pray in the Garden: "Father, if thou art willing, remove this cup from me; nevertheless not my will, but thine, be done" (Lk 22:42).

Thus God-made-man can traverse the fatal path in reverse; humbling himself to become a baby, a poor country carpenter, he can from perfect humility give perfect obedience. Then "the spell begins to work backward"; man's restoration to his original integrity has begun. What we call God's "grace" is the Holy Spirit fitting us first into the pattern of Christ's death, then into the pattern of his Resurrection.

The sermons preached by the first Christians were full of this idea. Christ was "obedient even unto death." He has risen, has ascended, and has sent us the Holy Spirit; our sins are to be forgiven if we accept him and live in his Spirit (for example, Acts 2:14, 40; 3:13–26; 13:16–41). Paul's Epistles are full of it, and so are the other Epistles. Paul explains the idea in many ways, depending on what ideas his audience was familiar with. To the Jews, he explains Christ's death as the fulfillment of the sacrifices of the Jewish Temple, where the killing of animals symbolized the complete offering of man's will and his possessions to God. To his gentile converts, he spoke in terms of freeing a slave from his slavery, ransoming a captive from his kidnappers.

But however he explains it, the essentials are the same: Christ was humble, Christ was obedient, Christ has risen, the Spirit has come. We must imitate Christ in his obedience, not by our own power but by the power of the Spirit within us.

In many ways unlike his Master in his *methods* of teaching (no parables, few of Christ's homely illustrations, etc.), Paul was like him in this: he would seize on an illustration and use one aspect of it, balancing it elsewhere with another illustration. (God, said Christ, is like the unjust judge: not, of course, in being unjust but in one respect—you must keep asking and asking. But again, God is like the prodigal son's father, who saw his son coming "a great way off" and went to forestall his request.) Thus Paul has suffered in the same way as his Master: men have taken one thread of his teaching and overemphasized it, ignoring the other threads and the whole pattern.

Thus Paul will talk at one time as if the "price" Christ paid was a literal money ransom paid to God, or even to Satan. At other times, the ransom idea is forgotten and Christ's death is the complete fulfillment of the Temple sacrifices. Elsewhere Christ is the guide who has pioneered the way we must follow, the heir who has shared his inheritance with us the adopted children, and so on. Some of the early Christian writers seized on one or the other of these illustrations and produced strange or even repugnant theories about the meaning of the Atonement. But even in them, there is often more balance than at first appears.

C. S. Lewis is right, of course, when in *Mere Christianity* he says that theories about the Atonement are of little importance in comparison with the fact of the Atonement. But we should seek to understand that fact as deeply and completely as we can, and we should reject silly or unworthy accounts of its meaning.

One source of uneasiness we can perhaps allay: that since Christ was God as well as man, somehow his example is too perfect, too remote from our struggles and failures, to be a guide for us. But of course if what we have said is correct, it is not a matter of mere external imitation; by the power of the Spirit, Christ is beginning to live in the Christian. One is tempted to use physical analogies, such as induction in an electrical coil or Coriolis force in a pump—one force carrying along another with it. But although living in Christ is not mere external imitation, it is voluntary; we can refuse to submit to the force. It will carry us along if we will let it.

Thus, on the traditional Christian view, our sins are our own; they are failures to open ourselves to God's grace, refusals to let that Life live in us. But to our virtues and accomplishments we can lay no real claim; we have merely stopped struggling and let Christ act in us. The accusation of wish fulfillment that sometimes haunts the back of our minds when we speak of the peace and joy that Christian faith brings breaks on this rock: the price of this peace and joy is complete self-surrender, the death of our merely natural self. The resurrection of that self is glorious, but that does not mean the crucifixion of the self is not terrible. It was terrible for Christ, and the servant is not greater than his master. But now the way has been blazed; like Saint Wenceslaus' page, we can walk in the great footsteps.

14

Organized Religion

Even if all that has been said up to now is granted, there still remains a difficulty about Christianity as "organized religion". In this chapter, I will defend organized religion as an ideal, but no one can defend it as it has so often been practiced. We Christians are the best arguments against Christianity. Our sins, our divisions, our uncharities, our timidity bring us under the dreadful condemnation of our Master. "By their fruits you shall know them", and our fruits are sour and scanty, where they exist at all. But "organized religion", like organized society or organized families, is not something we can do without. Anarchy is worse than even the worst societies, promiscuity is worse than even the worst marriages, and unorganized religion is worse than any sect or group sincerely trying for Christian community. This is because a Christian group that is not just a pretense has the promise that "where two or three are gathered in my name, there am I in the midst of them" (Mt 18:20). And little as we heed or help him, that promise does not altogether fail.

Let us first look at the need for "organized religion" and the form it would ideally take. The need is created by Christ's commands to his followers: "Go therefore and make disciples of all nations, baptizing them in the name of the Father and of the Son and of the Holy Spirit, teaching them to observe all that I have commanded you; and lo, I am with you always, to the close of the age" (Matthew 28:19–20). The mission of Christ's followers, in other words, is to *teach* certain truths, to *administer* baptism and the other sacraments, and to *preach* obedience to God's laws. *Knowing* the teaching, *using* the sacraments, *obeying* the commandments is the job of the whole Christian community, but from the earliest records of Christianity, some men were set aside from the rest of the community to teach God's truths, administer his sacraments, and preach his law. Thus we have the division into clergy and laity, and the need for support of the clergy. We also see developing very naturally places set aside for worship, an accepted order of service, and so on: what "church" means to many people.

Many Christians believe Christ intended the supper he gave to his apostles the night before he suffered to be repeated by the Christian community and that only those who have received the laying on of hands that descends from the first apostles can carry on this commemoration. There will then be two sacraments: the Communion itself and the ordination to perform this rite, which will be reserved for a special minority in the Church. These "professionals" have then tended to be entrusted with baptism, except in emergencies, though the Christian tradition has always been that any baptized person can baptize in case of need. They have also tended to witness marriages as representatives of the Christian community, and so on. Roman Catholics and Orthodox Christians believe that seven *sacraments* or special means of grace—baptism, confirmation, marriage, ordination, Communion, absolution for sins, and anointing of the sick and dying—were intended by Christ and taught by him to his disciples. Episcopalians hold that only baptism and

Communion are necessary for salvation, though many of them regard the other sacraments as instituted by Christ. Protestants of other denominations, for whom the written documents of Christianity are the only rule of faith, have found no ground in these documents for some of the seven.

If Christians are to pass on Christ's message, there must be some check on whether it is Christ's message or their own additions to it that they are passing on. If they are to administer his sacraments, there must be some agreement as to who is entitled to do so and what is to be done. If men are to be exhorted to keep God's laws, there must be some agreement as to what these are. If God's commands include exhortations to help those in need, as they do, then there will be a need for practical organization of such help. If meeting together for instruction, worship, and the Supper are natural expressions of Christian life or commanded by Christ, then meeting places and their administration will be necessary.

So Christianity becomes, and in the nature of the case must become, "organized religion". We find the process already going on in the Acts of the Apostles and in the Epistles, and it must surely have been intended and foreseen by Christ, even speaking purely on the natural and practical level. Most Christians, of course, believe he intended to form an organized community, a Church. They differ on the nature and present identity of that Church but not always as widely as it may seem to the outsider. They hold, with Paul, that the Church is in a real sense Christ's body, not only an organization but an organism moved by Christ's life.

Granted the necessity of organization, what sort of community is to be organized? Obviously a community united by love of God and of each other, dedicated to spreading

God's message and his reign, to using the sacraments to grow in Christ's life. The marks of this community in its early days are obvious: "Look how these Christians love one another."

Not only love, but joy and gaiety were notes of the early Christian community. Paul's "Rejoice in the Lord always; again I will say, Rejoice" (Phil 4:4) finds many echoes in the life and writings of the early Christians. The Christians went to the lions singing songs of joy, not dirges. "The fruit of the Spirit is love, joy, and peace" (Gal 5:22).

When we ask why this love and joy are not equally characteristic of modern Christians, we must begin by making a distinction. We must distinguish those who are officially Christian but have no real commitment to the teachings of Christ from those who make a serious effort to live by Christ's teaching. Among the committed Christians, the love, joy, and peace of the early Christians are still to be found. So our real question must be: "Why are so few official Christians committed Christians?"

The answer, I fear, is that a little Christianity, like a little knowledge, is a dangerous thing. An exposure to Christian doctrine taught by people who are themselves not excited by it, an exposure to people who go through the motions of Christian living without real commitment, can act like a vaccination to prevent any more serious "infection". On the other hand, those who have been exposed to Christians who are genuinely committed often catch the enthusiasm and become committed Christians themselves. The exposure need not even be by direct personal contact. It can come about through reading the New Testament or by reading the life or writings of some great Christian. Whether we give them a capital *S* and a halo or not, the Saints renew the vitality of Christianity in every age.

Something similar happens outside Christianity or out-side of religion altogether. A great teacher, a great artist, a great master in any field can draw people after him, inspire them with his enthusiasm. But of course, in these cases it is not surprising that some people do not become enthusias-tic, for no matter how great the teacher, science may not be your cup of tea; no matter how great the artist, you may not be inspired to imitate his artistic creation.

How can we explain, though, the indifference of so many official Christians? If Christianity is true, its message is for every man. All men are called to follow Christ, and only by following Christ can men find their true fulfillment. Many, of course, follow Christ without knowing him, but what of those who know him but do not follow him?

I suspect part of the answer is that the familiar trio of the world, the flesh, and the devil are firmly ensconced inside official Christianity as well as outside it. The churches have a great tendency to model themselves on the world about them rather than on the teachings of their Master. The Roman Catholic Church retains a sort of fossilized image of the hierarchy of the Roman Empire, and the Orthodox Churches retain the same sort of image of the Byzantine Empire. Some Protestant churches seem to retain the model of rural communities where the vicar and the gentry were in charge of the uneducated populace, while others pre-serve other patterns from their origin. Some churches seem modeled on successful businesses, using salesmanship to reach the "consumers" of religion, while others seem to model themselves on social service organizations.

Of course, where these are merely external impressions on a church, they are of little importance, though many sincere seekers after religious truth have been put off, tem-porarily or permanently, by the baroque protocol of Roman

Catholicism or the old-fashioned language of the Episcopalian service. The Pope carried in the sedan chair surrounded by peacock fans may be a humble and sincere man, but to the outsider he does not look it. The message expressed in sixteenth-century English may be vital and contemporary, but to the outsider it sounds remote and archaic.

Where the influence is not merely external—where, for example, visible affluence or success are valued instead of love of God and neighbor—then the influence will be still more deadly. And at all times there is great pressure on the Church simply to preach as Christianity whatever values the society of the time wants preached. Christianity has often been accused of this, and the accusation has too often been true. The values preached may sometimes be well enough in their place, as when a Christian missionary preaches soap and civilization. But the attempt to preach them under the name of Christianity ultimately discredits the substituted values as well as Christianity.

The temptations of the flesh in Christianity are not usually the spectacular ones. Greediness of all kinds is, I suspect, the major temptation, along with laziness. The comfortable, indeed, the overstuffed (in several senses of the word), Christian is uncomfortably familiar. And of course, nastiness of all sorts can take refuge under Christian masks: malice as righteous indignation, laziness or timidity as forbearance or benevolence, and so on. The overemphasis on sexual sins in some Christian churches has made some Christians feel that as long as they were chaste they could be gluttons or gossips, Scrooges or misery spreaders. And of course, prurience can masquerade as concern for our neighbors' morals.

But the greatest sins are, of course, spiritual. The frequency with which some sort of official adherence and outward conformity to Christianity has been made an excuse for spiritual pride and for hatred of others is depressing. When Christianity presents this face to the outsider or to the child growing up in a church, rejection of this perversion of Christianity may be the reaction closest to the spirit of Christ. Christians too easily forget that Judaism was the "true church" until the coming of Christ and that the Pharisees and Scribes have their modern equivalents in the "pillars of the church".

There are also, of course, intellectual failings. Some Christians under the onslaught of criticism from science and philosophy have tried to make their position unassailable and have succeeded only in emptying it of meaning. Others have succumbed to the temptations of irrationalism in faith: rejecting logic and evidence in favor of a mere will to believe, which would justify any belief as well as Christianity. A sort of misplaced humility and charity seems to have led some Christians to complete relativism, as if holding some proposition true and its denial false was a form of pride or saying that someone was wrong was a failure in charity. The idea of truth as a positive good, which we can thank God for giving us, undeserving as we are, and which we can try to share with those who lack it, seems to have dropped out of much modern Christianity. Some of these errors may be a sign of kindheartedness, but they are certainly also a sign of muddleheadedness.

What is the solution to the lack of true Christianity inside of official Christianity? I wish I knew. Of one thing I am fairly certain: no merely external reform or rearrangement will solve the problem. Abolishing "organized religion" will not solve it, for this will merely mean that some things that need to be done will be done badly or not at all. No liturgical reform or new system of catechetical instruction, no rearrangement of parishes or redeployment of clergy will in itself solve the problem, though of course any or all of these things may need to be done at one time or another.

I suspect that after all it is up to each individual Christian, first to reform his own life and then to use whatever talents and opportunities he has to reform the Church around him. It is not a new solution, and it may seem far less exciting than pushing some great scheme of reform. But it has the advantage of being the solution commanded by Christ. He still, as in life, is to be found in the company of sinners; and he still calls individuals to repent and renew their faith.

15

Last Things

Not very long ago the "four Last Things"—death, judgment, Heaven, and Hell—loomed large in the consciousness of most Christians. Some welcome the fact that this is no longer true, but perhaps mistakenly. As C. S. Lewis says:

> If you read history you will find that the Christians who did most for the present world were just those who thought most of the next. The Apostles themselves, who set on foot the conversion of the Roman Empire, the great men who built up the Middle Ages, the English Evangelicals who abolished the Slave Trade, all left their mark on Earth, precisely because their minds were occupied with Heaven. It is since Christians have largely ceased to think of the other world that they have become so ineffective in this. Aim at Heaven and you will get earth "thrown in"; aim at earth and you will get neither.[1]

If Lewis is right, we need an increased understanding of the traditional Christian beliefs about life after death, and a renewed interest in those beliefs. We have already briefly considered the importance of a belief in life after death in our discussion of the accusation that the Christian belief in

[1] *Mere Christianity* (San Francisco: Harper, 2001), p. 134.

God's love is meaningless because it cannot be disproved by any event (in chapter 1), and our discussion of Christianity as giving an adequate meaning and purpose to life (in chapter 11). But we need to take a more full-scale look at the subject.

Let us begin by looking at an accusation about the Christian teaching on life after death, the accusation that a belief in judgment, Heaven, and Hell renders ethics purely a matter of prudence. The bribe of Heaven and the threat of Hell, it is alleged, make it impossible for a Christian ethic to be anything but a matter of cunning calculation on the one hand and servile fear on the other. To answer this adequately, we will need to look at what Christians in fact believe about judgment, Heaven, and Hell.

The primary consideration in judgment, on the Christian view, is obedience to the two great commandments, love of God and love of neighbor. Love of God will find natural expression in love of neighbor. (John tells us that he who says he loves God and yet hates his neighbor is a liar.) Christ himself pictured the judgment in what C. S. Lewis called a "terrible parable" (Mt 25:31–46), for the unjust are condemned wholly on the basis of sins of omission: "I was hungry and you did not feed me, thirsty and you did not give me drink." We can, of course, think of this judgment as if the test and the reward were completely independent, but we will be nearer the truth if we regard them as necessarily connected. The man who is purely selfish will regard his fellow men merely as tools to be used for his own power and pleasure—things to be manipulated. He will regard God with complete detestation, for the absolute superiority of God, his omnipotence and wisdom, makes him the Great Rival, who cannot be bent to the selfish man's will, who has the power and knowledge that the selfish man covets for himself.

When a man of this type dies, he loses the power to manipulate and torment his fellow man, and he loses those reflections of God's goodness and glory that are the joys and delights of this world. He is faced with the choice of abandoning his own will and enjoying the Source of all joy, or of choosing his own will and rejecting God. But to reject God is to reject all joy and delight. The choice is God or nothing, and the damned soul chooses Nothing. According to the belief of most Christians, the damned also receive the punishment their individual sins have merited (what theologians call the "pain of sense"); they feel, for example, those pains they have inflicted on others, knowing (for self-deception is no longer possible) that they are receiving exactly the measure they themselves have meted out. But these punishments are of their nature limited. The real pain of Hell (what theologians call the "pain of loss") is that the damned have made themselves *unable* to enjoy the only Source of joy that ever existed or can exist. A certain removal from the hated Rival, the unendurable, hated Joy, may be a mercy that is granted.

The doctrine of Hell is a terrible one, but if freedom is real, Hell must be possible. As Lewis says:

> If a game is played, it must be possible to lose it. If the happiness of a creature lies in self-surrender, no one can make that surrender but himself (though many can help him to make it) and he may refuse. I would pay any price to be able to say truthfully "All will be saved." But my reason retorts, "Without their will, or with it?" If I say "Without their will" I at once perceive a contradiction; how can the supreme voluntary act of self-surrender be involuntary? If I say "With their will", my reason replies "How if they *will not* give in?" [2]

---

[2] *The Problem of Pain* (San Francisco: Harper, 2001), p. 120.

But terrible as the doctrine of Hell is, its misuse by some Christians is even more appalling. The blitheness with which some Christians consign those they disagree with or dislike to Hell, even taking satisfaction in the idea, is horrifying. Christ has told his followers to judge not lest they be judged, and he has warned them that the first shall be last and the last first. Aside from this, the Christian who genuinely loves God and his neighbor will see any soul going to Hell as a terrible blow to the Christian community, a defeat for God's plan. Some aspect of God's goodness will go forever unseen, unsung, unshared because of that loss. There will be empty places at the Great Feast, and though nothing can mar the joy of that celebration once we have come to it, until we do come to it the salvation of our neighbor should be our most serious and permanent concern. The Christian should be willing to do or suffer anything to prevent any soul from coming to that end. Paul wished he himself could be lost if it would save others. But of course, the charity that could seriously will such a loss makes it impossible.

Heaven, of course, is the exact reverse of Hell. In Christ's parable, it is probably the gentiles, the "nations", whose judgment is being pictured. The souls of the just seem not to have known that it was Christ they were serving ("When did we see You hungry and give You food?"), but their charity to others has been the thread that connected them, however tenuously, to the world of life and truth and love. Many Christians who were confident of their salvation will stand shamefaced enough on that day, barely saved ("the first shall be last"), and many who followed the Light of the World in strange guises and even thought themselves the enemies of that Light will enter into the Joy ("the last shall be first"). Sin will be no barrier if it is repented ("the whores and tax collectors will enter the Kingdom of Heaven before you [Scribes and Pharisees]").

Many Christians believe in some form of purification or "Purgatory" for all but the most perfect souls before the joy of Heaven can be entered. Misunderstandings and misuses of this doctrine have led to its rejection by many Protestant Christians, while others (C. S. Lewis for one) find some form of this idea acceptable.

For the souls who enter Heaven, their love of God (in whatever guise) and of their fellow man has been the preparation that makes Heaven possible for them, just as the souls who have hated God and neighbor have made Heaven impossible for themselves. Those who have learned to love goodness and to delight in it will find Goodness himself to love and delight in. Those who have delighted in truth will find Truth himself, the fount of all reality. Those who have loved beauty will delight forever in the Beauty "ever old and ever new" of God.

During their life on earth, their pursuit of goodness or truth or beauty may have been painful or severe. They may not have guessed that by developing a taste for reality, they have made themselves capable of joy. But those who have gone outside of themselves and learned to love or appreciate anything real have by that very fact made themselves able to delight in God.

We can see that what we have said about the nature of judgment, Heaven, and Hell enables us to cast additional light on some of the questions we discussed earlier. Consider, for example, the problem about the identity of the disembodied soul that we discussed in chapter 1. If each soul is created to appreciate and enjoy a particular aspect of the divine nature, then each individual will be unique. Even in this life, each individual will have a unique view of the universe, his own slant on it; and those who know that individual will be able to know something of this. And of course, there would be no point in duplicating this unique slant, creating another person with this view of the universe. Thus our doubts about the uniqueness of the individual soul can be laid to rest.

Similarly, if each individual's destiny after death is the direct outgrowth of the life he has lived on earth, then the specter of false memory after death can be laid to rest. Each of us will be judged, and know his judgment, if the Christian view is true; there will be no grounds for doubt that the person who is rewarded or punished is the same who earned that reward or punishment.

Indeed, there will be no room for doubt of anything at all. Paul says that now we see as in a glass darkly, but then we shall know as we are now known by God. Whatever this now unimaginable mode of knowledge is, it will leave no room for error, for in God's knowledge there is no error. So again the idea that there may be error or uncertainty after death must be false if Christianity is true. Presumably certain mystical experiences have been a preliminary hint or partial anticipation of this "knowing as we are known" (which theologians call the "Beatific Vision"), and these experiences seem to leave no possibility of doubt or uncertainty, any more than there is room for doubt or uncertainty that we are experiencing joy or pain while we are experiencing it.

What we said in chapter 11 about the Christian idea of Heaven as giving an adequate idea of the purpose of life also receives fuller illumination from our examination of the idea of Heaven. For that purpose can begin to be fulfilled in our present lives, as we grow in knowledge and love of God by serving him. This growth in knowledge and love will give us foretastes of that joy which our continual growth in knowledge and love after death will give us completely. So the quest for joy, too, fits into our developing picture.

Indeed, it is not too much to say that from the perspective of the Last Things, all that we have said previously comes together into one picture. Our search for God cannot be merely wishful thinking, for only a will cleansed of self-love and willing to give itself entirely to God can desire what is promised: It is safe to promise the pure in heart will see God, for only the pure in heart will want to. The function of pain and suffering in our lives becomes clear, for we can choose God over self only if there is some sacrifice of self in choosing God. The universe is designed to teach us the lesson of self-sacrificing love not because this is some arbitrary requirement on God's part but because only self-sacrificing love can enter into the only joy that is perfect. To ask God to give us some source of joy or satisfaction that does not involve this sort of love is to ask the impossible. He has nothing to give but himself. He gives himself partially and indirectly in this world and completely in the next. But the sort of giving of himself that involves free creatures necessarily involves a taking, an acceptance, on the part of those creatures. If we will take, he can give. If we will not take, he *cannot* give. Some do refuse, and thus there is Hell, which is the absence of God. As C. S. Lewis says:

> The whole dance, or drama, or pattern of this three-Personal life is to be played out in each one of us: or (putting it the other way round) each one of us has got to enter that pattern, take his place in that dance. There is no other way to the happiness for which we were made. Good things as well as bad, you know, are caught by a kind of infection. If you want to get warm you must stand near the fire: if you want to be wet you must get into the water. If you

want joy, power, peace, eternal life, you must get close to, or even into, the thing that has them. They are not a sort of prize which God could, if He chose, just hand out to anyone. They are a great fountain of energy and beauty spurting up at the very centre of reality. If you are close to it, the spray will wet you: if you are not, you will remain dry. Once a man is united to God, how could he not live forever? Once a man is separated from God, what can he do but wither and die? [3]

The natural law, which reason reveals in the universe, and the moral law, which reason finds in our hearts, were used earlier in this book to argue for the existence of God. And that, of course, is part of their purpose, to teach us that God exists and makes demands on us. But the scientist's delight in the intricate unity of natural law, the moralist's delight in the intricate unity of the moral law, the ordinary man's enjoyment of natural beauty and moral goodness are all hints and foretastes of that delight in God which is our destiny.

Our knowledge of and delight in God's revelation points in the same direction. Even something as minor and in its own way as unsupernatural as an enjoyment of church services, or of other aspects of organized religion, is a pointer of the same sort. Every good thing is a pointer back to the God from which it came, and no good thing is his rival. Only the misuse of good things, their perversion, can lead us away from God. And in leading us away from God, evil leads us away from every goodness and happiness.

No good, as we have said, is *naturally* the rival of God; each good is intended to lead back to him, and will if we let it. But any good, from the lowest to the highest, can be *made* into a rival of God. This includes, among other things,

[3] *Mere Christianity*, p. 156.

our own inadequate ideas of God. Our guide to the proper use of good things must be the moral law; as Chesterton said, we must thank God for the gift of wine by not drinking too much of it, thank God for the gift of sex by being faithful. The moral law may lead us to sacrifice good things, either because sacrifice is demanded by duty or charity or because we realize that we are in danger of becoming over-dependent on them, that they are leading us away from God.

But "the moral category exists only to be transcended", as Lewis has pointed out. Even now we can occasionally find ourselves doing what is right naturally and with enjoyment. The Roman Catholic marriage service reminds the bride and groom that "love makes sacrifice easy, perfect love makes it a joy", and we sometimes find ourselves proving this in our living. Even in Heaven, Lewis points out,

> we must remember that the soul is but a hollow which God fills. Its union with God is, almost by definition, a continual self-abandonment—an opening, an unveiling, a surrender of itself. A blessed spirit is a mold ever more patient of the bright metal poured into it, a body ever more completely uncovered to the meridian blaze of the spiritual sun. We need not suppose that the necessity for something analogous to self-conquest will ever be ended, or that eternal life will not also be eternal dying.... For in self-giving if any where we touch a rhythm not only of all creation but of all being. For the Eternal Word also gives Himself in sacrifice; and that not only on Calvary.... From before the foundation of the world He surrenders begotten Deity back to begetting Deity in obedience.... From the highest to the lowest self exists to be abdicated, and by that abdication, becomes the more truly self.[4]

[4] *The Problem of Pain*, pp. 156–57.

It is this abdication of self that the evil man on earth refuses and that the damned soul in Hell refuses finally. In this refusal, the evil man begins to lose joy and the damned soul loses it finally. It is this abdication that the suffering of this world makes possible and for which suffering exists in order to teach us. But even a little self-abdication wins us a foretaste of that joy which our complete self-abandonment in Heaven will bring us in full measure.

Meanwhile, the glory fades in our mind—and it is not meant to last, now—and we face again the workaday tasks of knowing and loving and serving God in a world that often does not look or feel like a world in which God is present. Our mind will be dazzled with sophistries, our belief dulled by habit. Our heart will be broken by sorrows, our will tempted by the world, the flesh, and the devil. Here we are pilgrims and travelers, but all is well with us if our feet are pointed homeward, if we believe, and act as if we believe, in the resurrection of the dead and life everlasting.

APPENDIXES

Justice, Mercy, and Atonement

Philosophy inherits from its beginnings certain characteristic approaches. From Socrates we inherit the practice of asking hard questions about even our most cherished beliefs and practices and of not being content with easy answers. From Plato we inherit the insight that we sometimes have to answer these hard questions by producing philosophical theories that go beyond already accepted ideas. From Aristotle we inherit the method of building up a philosophical system by paying careful attention to common sense (that is, the opinions of the many) and to previous philosophical theorizing (that is, the opinions of our predecessors).

Each philosophical tradition has its weaknesses. Socratic questioning may degenerate into scepticism if we reject reasonable answers to our hard questions. Platonic theorizing can turn into a sort of gnosticism that rejects common sense because of a conviction that the truth can never be in the opinions of the multitude. Aristotelian systematization can turn into a rigid orthodoxy more concerned to defend the accepted views than to be open to new truth.

When philosophers turn to philosophical theology, they bring to bear all of these traditions. We sometimes affront the pious by asking searching questions about the meaning and justification of cherished beliefs. We sometimes find ourselves theorizing beyond the letter at least of revelation in order to answer these hard questions. And we sometimes find ourselves making hard choices about how to fit revelation into our philosophical systems.

One of the most basic and cherished Christian beliefs, surely common to any religious view that can justifiably call itself Christian, is the idea of the Atonement: that Christ suffered and died to save us from our sins. Hostile philosophical critics have often attacked this basic belief as morally monstrous. More recently, some Christian philosophers have asked some hard Socratic questions about traditional understandings of the Atonement. For convenience I divide questions about the Atonement into three general categories: (1) is the idea of the Atonement contrary to *justice*, (2) is it contrary to *mercy*, and finally (3) is the idea even *intelligible*?

The objection from justice asks whether it is fair for one person to suffer for the sins of others, or fair for the others to benefit from the suffering of that one. The objection from mercy asks why the Atonement was even needed: Why could God not simply have forgiven us without the need for Christ's suffering and death? The objection from intelligibility asks if the idea of transferring merit or demerit from one person to another even makes sense.

In this essay, I give an answer to these difficulties that is Aristotelian in my sense rather than Platonic. In other words, I do not think that the way out of the difficulties raised is to come up with a new theory about the Atonement but rather to examine very carefully how the idea of atonement fits in with our basic moral intuitions and with the theories that earlier Christian philosophers and theologians have advanced. I try to elicit the moral intuitions by storytelling, by using the method of parable as thought experiment. And with regard to our predecessors' theories, I start off with the idea that very likely each of the historic theories is, as so often happens in philosophy, an exaggeration of a partial truth about the matter and that what is needed is to put these theories together into a synthesis in which each partial truth is related to the other to get at something that approaches the whole truth.

My own view is that the "Aristotelian" method is generally the proper one in both philosophy and theology. Our predecessors were not fools; they were unlikely to be wholly wrong in their theorizing. Where they disagree, it is unlikely that the truth lies wholly on one side. Similarly, our common moral intuitions may need some correction in the light of revelation or of philosophical theory, but they are unlikely to be wholly mistaken. In theology, any view that ignores or drastically revises the nearly twenty centuries of Christian belief and practice is by that very fact almost certainly mistaken. But perhaps that is only to say that I am basically Aristotelian in my philosophical outlook and orthodox in my Christianity. The questioners and the innovators must have a hearing before we can dismiss them.

The idea of the injustice of atonement is, I think, an attempt to appeal to certain moral intuitions. Is the appeal a successful one?

Consider the following parable:

A certain king had a jewel which he valued so highly that he had enlisted a band of knights, sworn to safeguard the jewel or die in the attempt. An enemy of the king, desiring the jewel, corrupted the knights one after another, some with bribes, some with threats, and some with promises. Then the enemy carried off the jewel. The king's son, who had been away with his squire while this was happening, returned to find the jewel gone. He went alone into the

enemy's stronghold and, after great suffering, managed to
get the jewel back. On his return, the king held court. The
foresworn knights came before him to express their sorrow
and accept their punishment. The king's son was also there,
and his father praised him for his heroism, promising him
whatever reward he wished. The prince said to the king,
"Father, as my reward I ask that you do not punish the
foresworn knights. Let my sufferings in getting back your
jewel be all that anyone has to suffer in this matter." The
king agreed, but the prince's squire objected, saying, "This
is to put these traitors on an equality with those of us who
have not betrayed their king." However, the chief of the
foresworn knights replied to him, saying, "Sir, we are not
on an equality with you but are below you in one way and
above you in another. You are above us in that you have
never betrayed your king, while we are forgiven traitors.
But we are above you in that our prince has given us a gift
that you have not received from him: his suffering has won
our pardon. Therefore we have more reason to love our
prince, and more motive to serve him and his father faith-
fully in the future."

It is tempting to elaborate this parable, but the bare bones I
have just given will be enough to make my points. First, it
seems to me that my own moral intuitions tell me that the
king's action was morally right, that the prince's action was
morally admirable, and that the chief knight's reply to the
squire was just. That is, to speak without parable, it is morally right to punish someone less than they deserve at the
request of someone who has done a supererogatory act,[1]
and this is not unfair to someone who has not deserved to
be punished: a person who does not deserve punishment has

---

[1] A *supererogatory act* is defined by the *Oxford English Dictionary* as "doing
more than duty requires".

no right to demand punishment for those who have deserved punishment if the person responsible for administering punishment has good reason to remit that punishment.[2]

If someone's moral intuitions disagree with this, it may be for one of several reasons. First, he may be a *strict retributionist*. A retributionist is one who holds that we can *deserve* punishment, and a strict retributionist is one who holds that we should never punish more or *less* than is deserved. Because deserving punishment and deserving reward are so closely linked, it would seem reasonable for a strict retributionist to also hold that we should never reward less or *more* than is deserved. Strict retribution can be contrasted with moderate retributionism, which is the view that we should never punish *more* than is deserved but may *for a good reason* punish less than is deserved. (And analogously, we may never reward less than is deserved but may for a good reason reward more than is deserved.)[3]

Now, whatever may be said in general about the merits of strict retributionism, it seems quite clear that historical Christianity has rejected strict retributionism and holds to a moderate retributionist view. The Christian God is *just* in that he never punishes more than we deserve or rewards less than we deserve, but he is *merciful* in that he sometimes punishes us less than we deserve and *generous* in that he sometimes rewards us more than we deserve. Note that

---

[2] I was pleased to find, after working out my own views, that many of my theses agree with things said in different language by Aquinas in the *Summa Theologica* (referred to hereafter as *ST*). On this point, see IIIa, q. 49, a. 4, reply obj. 2, and q. 48, a. 2, reply.

[3] I first made this distinction in print in these terms in my *Moral Dilemmas* (Belmont, Calif.: Wadsworth, 1985), p. 54. Aquinas plainly disagrees with the basic point; see *ST* IIIa, q. 46, a. 2 ad 3, and *ST* IIIa, q. 46, a. 3 ad 3. "The man who waives satisfaction ... acts mercifully, not unjustly."

for a moderate retributionist, justice and mercy are quite compatible: only a strict retributionist sees them as incompatible. (Strict retributionists also have problems about generosity: the only philosopher I know who inclines to strict retributionism is very puzzled by the parable of the vineyard and is inclined to hold that the householder acts *unjustly*.)

I want to make a few more points in terms of my parable: First, the prince was *not* punished, and a fortiori was not punished in place of the knights. Second, the prince, being innocent, was in a position to perform an act of supererogation: the knights, being guilty, were *not* in a position to perform such an act. Anything they did would be at best an act of *reparation*. If all of the knights had died in an effort to recover the jewel, they would have been doing *less* than they were obliged to do, since they were obliged not to let it be stolen while they lived in the first place.

On the other hand, the prince was in a position to perform an act of supererogation—something more than his position and duties required of him. This notion of supererogation is, I think, as essential to the philosophical understanding of Christianity as are the notions of justice and mercy, although *under that name* it is a less familiar idea. However, I think that when Christians speak of the "generosity" or the "goodness" of God, what they often have in mind is God's *supererogatory* goodness—the good he would not be unjust in leaving undone.

This, then, is my answer to the accusation of injustice. It is not unjust that Christ's sufferings benefit us; it is not unjust to Christ because he was not *punished* for our sins but voluntarily did a supererogatory act in order to counteract the effects of our sins. It is not unjust that we benefit from Christ's sufferings, because we recognize in parallel cases the justice of allowing one person to be pardoned because of the supererogatory act of another.

Let us now turn to the difficulty involving mercy. One might feel that the king should show mercy *whether or not* the prince does any supererogatory act or makes any request. This seems to amount to the view that it is right to punish less than deserved without a good reason, or perhaps that repentance in itself is always a good reason, a view we might call *weak retributionism*.

"After all," one might say, "why shouldn't the king *simply* rescue and pardon the knights? Or if he needs a reason, why isn't the request of his son reason enough? Why should the son go through this elaborate charade to get his father to pardon the knights?"

The answer I would give is this: simple pardon or pardon at the mere request of the prince would give the knights a false idea of the seriousness of their sin and not give them the motive for repentance that the prince's sacrifice gives them. And *unless* the knights take their sin seriously and repent of *that* sin, the sin seen as serious, the king cannot forgive them. For forgiving, I would maintain, has a *logical* relation to a request for forgiveness. I *cannot* forgive you, nor you me, "unilaterally". I can express my readiness to forgive you, keep bitterness and hatred against you out of my heart, and we sometimes loosely call this "forgiveness". But genuine forgiveness is "at-one-ment", and it requires action on *both* sides. God's forgiveness of us is purely supererogatory: he would not be unjust if he did not forgive us. Our forgiveness of others is *not* supererogatory, since God, who has placed us under a debt of obligation, by being prepared to forgive us for his Son's sake, has *commanded* us to forgive each other and made our forgiveness of each other a *condition* of his forgiving us. This being so, it is odd to maintain that unconditional forgiveness is essentially superior to conditional forgiveness, and it is not clear that we are commanded to forgive without conditions. Certainly the *logical* condition of being asked for forgiveness always obtains.

But consider a wife who has been repeatedly beaten by her husband. Does Christian morality require her to continue living with the husband simply because after each incident he makes a verbal profession of sorrow and asks forgiveness? Consider a teenager who has been allowed to use the family car and has repeatedly disobeyed traffic laws, driven after drinking, and overstayed curfews. Should he be given the family car again simply because he makes a verbal request for forgiveness?

The point here is that forgiveness is not a license to continue with behavior that needs forgiving. The wife may well say to the abusive husband, "I forgive you, but I will not live with you unless you begin and stick with a course of therapy." The parents may say, "We forgive you, but you may not use the car again for several months."

This is quite in line with traditional Christian beliefs and practice: for example, a criminal might be regarded as sincerely repentant but still punished for his crimes. Repentance is certainly a *reason* for punishing less than deserved, but it is a reason that may be overridden; forgiveness is quite consistent with punishing exactly as much as is deserved.[4]

So my answer to the objection from mercy is that weak retribution makes an equal and opposite error to strict retributionism: by saying that we, or God, should not punish someone for no good reason, or merely because someone

---

[4] See *ST* IIIa, q. 52, a. 8, where the point is raised with regard to souls in Purgatory, who are not necessarily released from due punishment by Christ's passion.

expresses sorrow, we are ignoring both the seriousness of deserving punishment and the tendency of human nature not to take sin seriously if it is forgiven without anyone paying the price. Suppose, for example, the prince in our parable had done nothing and the king simply said to the knights, "I will not punish you; I have another jewel to guard and will put you in charge of it." Is the second jewel likely to be guarded even as well as the first one? To simply remit punishment without anyone suffering is to encourage repeated transgression and "cheap repentance".

That, of course, is the half truth exaggerated by strict retributionism, while the half truth exaggerated by weak retributionism is the insight that it is just to punish less than deserved. Strict retributionism has an excess with respect to justice and a defect with respect to mercy; weak retributionism has a defect with regard to justice and an excess with regard to mercy. Either view, if adopted, would greatly increase the burdens of trying to live morally—strict retributionism by making it too hard on the transgressor, weak retributionism by making it too easy on the transgressor (and too hard on the transgressor's victims). Both views are practical fallacies as well as intellectual fallacies.

Thus the alleged objections from justice and mercy do not, I think, call for any new approach to or theory about the Atonement, only a more careful analysis of our intuitions about justice and mercy, with some assistance from the concept of supererogation.

Let me turn now to traditional theories about the Atonement. Are any of them satisfactory? Do even the best of them involve some idea of transferring merit from one person to another that we cannot make sense of? (Of course, an incompatibility with a specific view of morality would be a two-edged sword: if we cannot fit a theory of the

Atonement into Kantian ethics, let us say, this might be a reason for abandoning Kantian ethics rather than abandoning that theory of the Atonement.)

One traditional theory of the Atonement is sometimes presented as what I will call a *strict retributionist view* of the Atonement and often, though not always, goes with a strict retributionist view in general ethics. On a strict retributionist view, the idea of the Atonement goes something like this: punishment has been deserved, God's justice will not allow simply ignoring the fact that punishment is deserved, so Christ is punished in our place. As I said earlier, I think that strict retribution is a profoundly unchristian view and that this view of the Atonement leads to the mistaken view that Christ was *punished* for our sins, a view quite different from the view that Christ *suffered* for our sins.[5]

Another theory of the Atonement that seems to me unsatisfactory is the *exemplary theory*: that in suffering and dying for us, Christ was *only* giving us an example of how God wants us to behave. Certainly Christ was doing at least this, giving us the supreme example of self-sacrificing love. But if we say that this is *all* he was doing, a problem arises. Christ could certainly have avoided suffering and dying, even by nonmiraculous means. So unless his suffering and death achieved some good that could best be achieved by those means, what example is Christ giving us—the example of undergoing *useless* suffering and death? Surely that is absurd. Yet if Christ's suffering and death were not useless, what were they useful for?

My suggestion at the beginning of this essay was that in suffering and dying, Christ was giving God a *good reason* to

---

[5] Aquinas clearly disagrees with this; he holds God could have forgiven us without any satisfaction for sin. See *ST* IIIa, q. 46, a. 3, ad 3.

punish us less and reward us more than we deserve on our own merits. His suffering and death for our sake give us a *claim* on God's mercy and generosity. God became a man; as a man, he offered his suffering and death for our sake. God now has *good reason* to show us justice and mercy.

We, on our part, should realize that we *owe* our forgiveness to the self-sacrificing act of love by Christ. We see that our salvation was costly, that someone suffered and died to earn it. If God in his own nature had merely forgiven us without it costing anyone anything, we would not have the same motive for gratitude and repentance: we do not value what seems easy. And in one very good sense, it would be easy for God to merely forgive us without anyone paying the cost.[6]

The language of "paying the cost" reminds us of a third theory of redemption, the *ransom theory*. Scorn has been heaped on this theory as being "primitive" or "naïve", but it is important to remember that this is the only theory that has some claim to support from Christ's own words. In Matthew 20:28, he says, "The Son of man came not to be served but to serve, and to give his life as a ransom for many." A ransom is a payment that gives a captor good reason to release a captive. If someone ransoms us from a captivity we have gotten into by our own fault, we have reason to be profoundly grateful to him and to do whatever we can in return.[7]

---

[6] For Aquinas, this is the major reason why God did not forgive us without satisfaction. See *ST* IIIa, q. 46, a. 3, reply, *Primo*. Notice that this is typically Aquinas' *first* response.

[7] See *ST* IIIa, q. 48, a. 4, and q. 49, a. 2. It should be noted that the paradigm case of ransom for us is ransom paid a kidnapper, but the paradigm case of ransom for the ancients and the medievals was ransom for a prisoner of war, who had typically surrendered, thus giving a commitment to his captors. This metaphor suggests that in the war against evil, we have laid down our arms and surrendered and are thus in a sense committed to evil or to its representative, Satan.

The puzzling part of ransom theories is how to answer the question, "Who was our captor?" To say "Satan" seems bad theology; to say "God" returns us to the picture of the strict retributionist God we rejected earlier. To say we were captives of "sin" is good New Testament language, but sin is not a personal agent who can be given a *reason* to release us.

One possible answer is that we were in a sense captives of *ourselves*, of our own self-enslavement to sin, an inability to turn ourselves around. Christ's suffering and death, then, give *God* a motive to give us the grace to repent and change our lives. In terms of our parable, suppose that the foresworn knights had in shame and despair surrendered to the enemy and been locked *into* his dungeon. The prince's sacrifice would give his father a good reason to use his power to free the knights from the imprisonment, which they could no longer do themselves.

The New Testament teaching that we are somehow incorporated into Christ gives us a hint as to how we might deepen our parable: the prince locks *himself* in the dungeon with the knights, and when the king rescues him, he rescues the knights as well. In this deepening of the parable, the jewel has a different importance: it is merely the symbol of and occasion for the knights' allegiance. The parable might begin:

> A certain king had a group of knights whom he loved. To give them a focus for their loyalty, he formed them into a brotherhood sworn to defend a jewel or die in the attempt. An enemy of the king, jealous of the loyalty of these knights, corrupted them ...

Perhaps in this parable the enemy destroys the jewel, making it *impossible* for the knights to restore it. The enemy is the jailor, and the shamed knights have let him imprison them. What the prince does is put himself voluntarily into the power of this jailor, then form a new brotherhood in the jail, of those who want to return to their former allegiance. In his name the new brotherhood sends a message to the king, asking for mercy; the king defeats the enemy and releases his son and the other captives. We need not change the ending of the parable; the prince and his squire and the leader of the knights speak as before.

But the problematic idea here is the idea of our *incorporation* into Christ: of our being part of the "body of Christ". If this is mere metaphor, what is it a metaphor for? If it is not pure metaphor, how can we make sense of it? Some philosophers and theologians have found a "legal fiction" interpretation of the metaphor satisfactory: God looks at us in our sinfulness but pretends to see Christ in his perfect obedience; our "filthy rags" are covered with the cloak of his righteousness. But so far as I can see, this interpretation (which is itself a metaphor, so we are interpreting a metaphor by a metaphor) fails because the idea of God "pretending" or "deeming" is unintelligible. The way God sees things is the way they are; the way God acts toward things is and must be based on the reality of these things.

A more attractive and innovative theory is Charles Williams' *theory of coinherence* (eagerly adopted by C. S. Lewis).[8] In the Williams view, our incorporation in Christ is a particular application of a general "spiritual law" that there are certain things that can be done for us *only* by others and

---

[8] On Williams' views, see Mary McDermott Shideler, *The Theology of Romantic Love* (Grand Rapids, Mich.: Eerdmans, 1962), passim, and especially chap. 8. On Lewis' attitude, see, for example, the material quoted in my *C. S. Lewis' Case for the Christian Faith* (San Francisco: Ignatius Press, 2004), pp. 55–60.

that we can do only for others, not ourselves. This theory needs a much more detailed discussion than I can give it here: it is immensely suggestive but perhaps merely restates the problem rather than solving it: *Why* are there things we can do only for others? *Why* is it a "spiritual law"? And even if it is a spiritual law in some areas, is not deserved punishment something that is nontransferable?

It seems that there is no real substitute for a theory of our incorporation into Christ that takes our unity with Christ as a genuine metaphysical fact. Just as an act done by my hand is an act done by me, so an act done by a member of Christ's mystical body is done by Christ, and an act done by Christ is an act done by his mystical body.[9]

This taking the unity of the mystical body has one seemingly embarrassing consequence and two welcome ones. The seemingly embarrassing consequence is that since members of Christ's mystical body sin, the body sins. But perhaps this makes sense of Paul's violent metaphor that Christ was "made sin for us."[10] The sins of the members become the sins of the body, just as the debts of a member of a family become family debts.

But equally, if a family member's debts become family debts, the family assets become the family member's assets. This means that we have a real right to the merits that Christ has deserved: as members of his body, these merits *belong* to us.

Even more crucially, the sufferings of members of the body become the sufferings of the body. Christ's mystical body suffers not only in Christ's own sufferings but in the

[9] 2 Cor 5:21. Aquinas makes this his principal explanation of how and why atonement works. See *ST* IIIa, q. 48, a. 1, reply, and q. 49, a. 1, ad 1.

[10] See *ST* IIIa, q. 8, a. 3 ad 2, where Aquinas deals with the sinfulness of the Church as an objection to Christ's "headship" of the Church.

sufferings of the starving baby, the old man dying of can-
cer, and the woman who is raped and murdered. And *all*
this suffering is redemptive; the crucifixion of Christ is
going on right now in the children's wards of hospitals, in
Mother Teresa's hospices for the dying, in the streets of
our cities. All suffering undeserved by the sufferer and freely
accepted out of love is an act of supererogation that gives
God a good reason to punish members of Christ's body
less than they deserve and to reward them far beyond their
individual merits.

In fact, we are no longer judged as individuals, in one
sense, at all: the body of Christ is judged, and judged worthy
of glory. The only way of cutting ourselves off from this
glory is to cut ourselves off from the body, which is what
serious sin does. But unlike a cell of a natural body, we
can be revivified once cut off from the body and be reunited
to it.

In fact, the life of Christ in us as members of his body,
which in some theological traditions is called sanctifying
grace, is precisely what makes us share in Christ's merits.
Many of us are still infected by and corrupted by sin, just as
in Christ's passion many of the cells of his natural body
were bruised, damaged, and filled with the poisons of fatigue
and trauma yet continued to live with his life. Some of us
die to Christ's life and fall away from the mystical body, just
as some cells of Christ's physical body died and fell away.

This whole picture of the essential unity of individual
human beings in Christ's mystical body will be profoundly
unsympathetic to many moderns. But taking it as a reality
and not just as a metaphor is the only way to resolve the
ultimate problems of sin and suffering. The pattern should
not be unfamiliar. In many philosophical problems bearing
on religion, we can go quite a long way using everyday

categories and judgments. For example, some suffering is obviously deserved, some obviously remedial or "soul-making". But there is always a "surd", like the sufferings of infants who die without any opportunity to learn or grow. This surd can be dealt with *only* by the full depths of Christian revelation. There are no *purely* philosophical answers to the deepest human problems, which is just to say that philosophy is not a substitute for religion.

What philosophy can do, however, is to show how much of revelation corresponds to our deepest human instincts, how many apparent conflicts between reason and revelation rest on confusions that can be solved by purely philosophical distinctions and arguments. But there comes a point at which philosophy can say only, "This problem is either insolvable, or it is solvable by this revealed doctrine." We are always free to reject the revealed doctrine: that is why faith is a virtue. But the price we pay for rejecting the revelation is that we are left with an insoluble problem. Either the sufferings of the innocent are part of the redemptive suffering of Christ's mystical body or there is no explanation of the sufferings of the innocent. And if there is no explanation of the sufferings of the innocent, God is not good, and we should not worship or serve God.

Thus, philosophical theology often points beyond itself.[11] It cannot give ultimate solutions to problems that can be

----

[11] Again, see Aquinas, *ST* Ia, q. 1, a. 1. Of course, it is quite legitimate for even Christian philosophers to deal with those parts of philosophy where the "handmaiden" is "mistress in her own house", that is, those parts of natural theology or general philosophy where purely philosophical reasons can be given for conclusions reached. But in my view, this unduly restricts us in philosophy of religion: see my *Thinking About Religion* (Englewood Cliffs, N.J.: Prentice Hall, 1978), pp. 23–28 passim, 150–51.

solved only by revelation. But it can indicate the gap in our understanding that only that revelation can fill. In this sense, philosophical theology can give us reason to believe, even where it cannot give us philosophical reasons to believe. That is both the limitation and the glory of natural theology: it is a handmaiden, but it is the handmaiden of the queen.

Chesterton, the Wards, the Sheeds, and the Catholic Revival

In the early 1950s, I was coming out of Foyle's bookstore on Charing Cross in London when I saw a rather surprising sight. In a blind alley between two parts of Foyle's was a small folding platform, rather like a stepstool with a tall railing on one side. On the railing was a crucifix and a rectangular sign on which was painted in rather faded gold letters, "Catholic Evidence Guild". Standing on the platform, leaning on the railing, was a young man who was speaking with an Australian accent about the Catholic faith. He was surrounded by a small crowd whose members frequently interrupted him with questions and objections.

As I walked over to the platform, the young man was arguing about free will with an older man in the crowd. In light of later knowledge, I imagine that they had gotten onto the topic by way of the problem of evil and the argument that a good deal of the evil in the world is due to human misuses of free will. The man in the crowd was defending determinism, denying that we have free will, and I was not entirely satisfied with the young man's reply. I do not remember if I intervened in the argument, but after

the young man had finished speaking and come down from
the platform, I buttonholed him and said something like
this: "Why didn't you refute what he was saying by telling
him that if determinism were true, he was determined by
causes beyond his control to believe in determinism and
you were determined by causes beyond your control not to
believe in it, so there would be no use arguing?"

I think my thought was something along the lines of C. S.
Lewis' argument against naturalism in *Miracles*: since the man
did think there was some use in arguing, this in itself was
an argument against determinism. The young man with the
Australian accent, whose name turned out to be Tony
Coburn, replied amicably that he was trying to convince
the man, not just refute him, and we got into an interesting
discussion.

Presently Tony said, "Some of us are planning to have
some tea at a shop near here. Why don't you join us?" I
then saw that some of the crowd were still waiting nearby
and were evidently friends or associates of Tony's. We went
to the tea shop, and over tea and cakes I discovered that my
companions were all speakers or prospective speakers for
the Catholic Evidence Guild, a group mostly composed of
Catholic laypeople who explained and defended Catholic
doctrine at street-corner meetings like the one I had just
observed.

I told them in turn that I was a recent convert to Catholicism, currently serving in the U.S. Army in England, and
on weekend leave in London. My own conversion had been
due in great part to reading the work of G. K. Chesterton.
I had encountered him first through a Father Brown story
in a collection of detective stories for children that I had
found in the children's room of the local library. Afterward
I had read the rest of the Father Brown stories, read much

of the rest of Chesterton's fiction, and then gone on to his essays. By absorbing G. K. Chesterton's intellectual progress into the Church, I explained that I had become convinced to follow his footsteps.

Somewhere in the midst of this explanation, an older lady in the group said, "Oh, I see you have my book." The book in question was Maisie Ward's *Return to Chesterton*, a supplement to her major biography of Chesterton. Wondering if the lady was a trifle dotty because she thought that my book belonged to her for some reason, I said that I had just bought the book at Foyle's.

Someone in the group laughed and said, "She means that she wrote the book. This is Maisie Ward." I think I was a little suspicious at first that my leg was being pulled, as the English say. But my conversation with the lady soon convinced me that she was indeed Maisie Ward, and I tried to convey some of my appreciation for her biography of Chesterton, which had helped me to see his life and thought in perspective.

Toward the end of this conversation, Maisie said, "You know, with your interests, you should really join the CEG." Not making the connection with the sign I had seen on the platform, I said, "Oh, is there a Chesterton society in London?" thinking vaguely that the *C* stood for Chesterton. I soon learned that the CEG was the way most of its members referred to the Catholic Evidence Guild, that there was a training program for speakers on Saturday nights, and that I was more than welcome to attend and see if it might be my cup of tea.

The last name in my essay title is Sheed, and although Maisie wrote under her maiden name, she was Mrs. Frank Sheed, co-owner with her husband of the Anglo-American publishing firm of Sheed and Ward. Saint Paul said you can have many teachers but only one father in the faith; Chesterton was my "father", but Frank and Maisie were certainly my "godparents" in the faith. I owe a very great deal of my happiness, my sanity, and such sanctity as I have managed to Gilbert, Maisie, and Frank; my life has been immeasurably richer because of them. The only comparable influence on me has been that of my older bother in Christianity, C. S. Lewis.

The meeting with Maisie just described was tremendously influential on my own life; without it and the meetings that followed, I might not be a philosopher, a teacher, and a writer today. But it also gave me some insights into the Catholic revival in England, and it is these I want to share with you.

Maisie's father and grandfather had been major influences on the nineteenth-century Catholic revival and had been friends of Newman and Manning. Maisie first met G. K. Chesterton at one of her father's parties for promising young writers. The publishing firm Sheed and Ward was founded about the time Maisie married Frank Sheed, a young Australian lawyer and Catholic activist who was to be a major intellectual influence on Catholicism in the English-speaking world. There was, in fact, in England and America a type of Catholic whom I always considered to be a "Sheed and Ward" Catholic, because their view of Catholicism was in line with and often influenced by the kind of books Sheed and Ward published. Often readers of Sheed and Ward books went on to be Sheed and Ward authors, as I might have myself when I began writing books other than textbooks if Sheed and Ward had still existed as it had been in its earlier days.

The chief characteristics of Sheed and Ward Catholicism were a deep love of the Church, which did not preclude a keen awareness of the Church's failings; a keen intellectual interest in the teachings of the Church; and a great ability to *enjoy* the life of faith and the life of reason. Some of the best discussions I have had and some of the most uproariously good times were with the members of the Catholic Evidence Guild, which was in many ways an extension of the Sheed and Ward apostolate.

Apostolate is an important word here. As publishers, and as moving spirits in the Catholic Evidence Guild, Frank and Maisie were taking very seriously our Lord's command to "go and teach all nations." That people should understand the Catholic faith, and knowing it, learn to love it, was the aim of their lives, as in many ways it was the aim of Chesteron's later life. Maisie Ward was, as I have said, a rather dowdy, older Englishwoman who was genuinely shy and modest but whose keen intellect, wide interests, and enthusiasm for her current projects were extremely impressive once you got to know her. Her daughter, Rosemary, who was a strikingly attractive young woman, gave some idea of what Maisie might have been like as a young woman.

Maisie's grandfather William G. Ward had been a friend of John Henry Newman and had preceded him into the Catholic Church. Indeed, Ward had a considerable influence on Newman's decision to move to the Roman Church, although they later quarreled. Maisie's father, Wilfrid Ward, was to become the editor of the *Dublin Review*, an influential journal of opinion, and later a biographer of Newman and others.

Maisie's mother, Josephine, was a member of the old Catholic aristocracy of England, those who had not changed their religion at the time of the Reformation. Through her Maisie was related to such members of the nobility as the Duke of Norfolk. More importantly, Josephine Ward, a highly intelligent woman who shared and encouraged her husband's intellectual interests, was a writer herself and became one of the early speakers for the Catholic Evidence Guild, bringing Maisie into the guild with her.

Wilfrid Ward cannot be said to have "discovered" Chesterton in the early days of Chesterton's career, but he certainly encouraged and admired him. Wilfred's article "Mr. Chesterton among the Prophets" is still one of the most intelligent and balanced assessments of Chesterton, though it was largely about Chesterton's early magnum opus, *Orthodoxy*.

It is interesting to read Chesterton's appreciation of Wilfrid Ward (as quoted by Josephine in a biographical note on her husband, Wilfrid, after his death):

> One admirable quality he had which is exceedingly difficult to describe ... I know not whether to call it a curiosity without restlessness, or a gigantic intellectual appetite rather amplified than moderated by patience. It is common to say of a man so acute that he had a restless activity of mind; for in the effort to evade the platitudes of praise a phrase like "restless" has almost become a compliment. But the mind of Wilfred Ward had very notably a restless activity. Thinking was to him like breathing. He never left off doing it; and he never thought himself remarkable for doing it; indeed so massive was his modesty and unconsciousness that he very often thought (quite erroneously) that his friends and acquaintances were doing it more than he was.
>
> Wilfred Ward was a biographer in a sense as exact as and more exalted than we apply to a biologist; he really dealt with life and the springs of life. Some are so senseless as to associate the function with merely indirect services to literature like those of the commentator and the bibliographer. They level the great portrait-painter of the soul with the people who put the ticket on the frame or the number in the catalogue. But in truth there is nothing as authentically

creative as the divine act of making another man out of the very substance of oneself. Few of us have vitality enough to live the life of another. Few of us therefore can feel satisfied with our own competence in or for biography, however fertile we may be in autobiography. But he was so full of this disinterested imagination of the biographer that even his short journalistic sketches were model biographies. He made a death-mask in wax with the firmness of a sculptor's monument in marble.

Yet I think the very positive qualities of his personality can perhaps still be most easily handled and summarized as those which made him so fine a critic of others. In his interpretations of Newman or of William George Ward he was without a suspicion of self-display; but he achieved something quite other and stronger than self-effacement. In truth, a magician needs a higher power of magic in order to disappear. But he did something very much more than disappearing. He was anything but merely receptive, he could be decidedly combative; but he could also, and above all, be strongly co-operative with another's mind. His intellectual qualities could be invisible because they were active, when they were the very virile virtues of a biographer which are those of a friend.[1]

Incidentally, it is those very virtues of Wilfrid Ward, inherited by his daughter, that make her biography of Chesterton such a major achievement. She was indeed a friend as well as a biographer, and with all respect to the achievements of other biographers, her biography gave us a picture of the essential Chesterton that is corrected or enhanced only in detail by later biographers. If one were to read only one biography of Chesterton, it should be Maisie's.

[1] Quoted in Mrs. Wilfrid (Josephine) Ward, *Last Lectures by Wilfrid Ward* (Freeport, N.Y.: Books for Libraries Press, 1967), pp. xv–xvii.

In her biography, Maisie may seem superficially to be a mere friend and admirer of Chesterton, but there is plenty of criticism of his weaknesses. However, I know from my own experience of writing about Lewis and Tolkien that if you write with approval, even tempered approval, of a controversial writer, those who dislike and disagree with that writer will dismiss your writing as mere propaganda by an admirer of the writer in question. The only kind of book about the author such critics will praise as "balanced" is a debunking or demolition of the writer.

All four Wards—W. G., Wilfrid, Josephine, and Maisie—were contributors to and encouragers of the Catholic revival in England in the nineteenth and twentieth centuries, especially insofar as this revival was an intellectual and literary phenomenon: Catholicism becoming intellectually respectable among the intelligentsia and Catholic writing becoming recognized as interesting and worthy of respect by the literary establishment. To appreciate their achievement, you have to know something of the contempt with which Catholic writing was treated by non-Catholics in England before this Catholic revival.

Chesterton was certainly one of the stars of the later Catholic revival, though he was not to be received into the Catholic Church until fourteen years before his death. And Chesterton always communicated with the ordinary person, through his newspaper columns, through his lectures, and toward the end of his life through radio broadcasts. But that person who did more than anyone except Chesterton himself to bring the Catholic revival to the ordinary intelligent person was not a member of any intellectual or literary elite. He was Maisie's Australian husband, Frank Sheed. Frank was a man of tremendous brilliance, vitality, and good humor. As a lecturer and street-corner speaker, Frank conveyed his excitement with and enjoyment of the truths of the Catholic faith. His books also manifested the beautiful clarity of his mind and a lucidity rivaled only by C. S. Lewis. But to know Frank only through his books was to miss a great deal.

As a publisher, Frank had the same virtues that Maisie and her father had as biographers: after introducing readers to his authors, he then stepped into the background. In the case of his French and German and Italian authors, this meant getting them translated into English (often more lucid than the original) and presenting them as part of an intellectual context in which the virtues on one writer balanced the faults of another.

In the case of English and later American writers, it was often a matter of seeing what would speak to the audience. For many English intellectuals, Father Ronald Knox's wartime sermons to the schoolgirls at the convent school, where he was quartered to carry on his scholarly work, seemed embarrassingly childish, even "cute" in a bad sense. Frank had the wit to see that the simplicity and directness of these books was precisely what many readers needed, and *The Creed in Slow Motion*, *The Mass in Slow Motion*, etc., may have illumined and inspired more minds than Knox's more "respectable" works ever did. Wilfrid Sheed, the son of Frank and Maisie and himself a writer of considerable range and diversity, has written a warm and illuminating picture of his parents. In this book, Wilfrid Sheed shows how the lecturing done by Frank and Maisie in effect created the audience for the books they would later publish. This audience of "Sheed and Ward Catholics" in turn formed the basis for many movements in Catholicism, in effect passing on the Catholic revival to the next generation.

The characteristics of this next generation of the Catholic revival in England and the United States were largely the characteristics I listed: love of the Catholic faith, intellectual excitement at the truths of the faith, and a feeling of joy in living the faith. These traits carried over in many of this "next generation" into Catholicism activism, the fight against racial injustice, efforts to help the poor and homeless at home and abroad, and activism in the cause of peace. Maisie, in particular, was involved in all of these efforts. Frank was completely behind her, but his own efforts were largely directed toward the intellectual underpinnings of these movements: writing, publishing, and lecturing on those things that had to be understood in order to moderate and direct activism.

The fading—I will not say the failure, but certainly the decline—of the Catholic revival came because too many people lost sight of these intellectual foundations. The decline began, I believe, when Catholics joined the fight against racial injustice and began deferring, for the very best of motives, to other leaders in the movement, letting them set tone and strategy. It was certainly a dilemma; to insist on their Catholic motivations and foundations for objecting to racial injustice might have seemed to others in the movement to be separatist or patronizing: "I will help you in your struggle, but on my terms, not yours." To avoid this predicament seemed to be an obvious good, but it set a dangerous precedent.

When Catholics began getting involved in other movements, such as the peace movement, they fell victim to a pattern that I will call the "more revolutionary than thou" syndrome, by which in any revolutionary movement the extremists tend to take over on the pretense that anyone who is not as extreme as they are is a traitor to the movement. It is the operation of this syndrome that has led, for example, to the women's movement for sexual justice being influenced and led by lesbians and separatists out of all proportion to their numbers in the movement or to the number of women who agree with their aims. The syndrome can be resisted; the American union movement has largely resisted it. But it has separated more than one movement for change from its base of supporters, and in a number of cases it has turned out that at least some of the extremists were in the pay of those opposed to change and had as their aim the alienation of the leaders of the movement from their rank-and-file supporters.

The effect of this syndrome on the Catholic revival was this: Catholics, excited by their faith, wanted to apply that faith to the needs of the world. To do so, they allied themselves with groups who regarded the righting of certain injustices or the meeting of certain needs as so self-evidently right that Catholicism was only a *means* to an end, and if Catholicism came into conflict with those ends, it was Catholicism that must give way.

It is precisely the situation described by C. S. Lewis in letter 7 of *The Screwtape Letters*, where Screwtape, the senior devil, advises the junior devil, Wormwood, as to how to undermine the newfound Christianity of the men Wormwood is tempting:

> Any small coterie, bound together by some interest which other men dislike or ignore, tends to develop inside itself a hothouse of mutual admiration, and towards the outer world, a great deal of pride and hatred which is entertained without shame because the "Cause" is its sponsor and it is thought to be impersonal.
>
> Whichever he adopts, your main task will be the same. Let him begin by treating the Patriotism or the Pacifism as part of his religion. Then let him, under the influence of partisan spirit, come to regard it as the most important part.

Then quietly and gradually nurse him onto the stage at which the religion becomes merely part of the "cause", in which Christianity is valued chiefly because of the excellent arguments it can produce in favor of the British war-effort or of Pacifism. The attitude which you want to guard against is that in which temporal affairs are treated primarily as material for obedience. Once you have made the World an end, and faith a means, you have almost won your man, and it makes very little difference what kind of worldly end he is pursuing. Provided that meetings, pamphlets, policies, movements, causes, and crusades, matter more to him than prayers and sacraments and charity, he is ours- -and the more "religious" (on those terms) the more securely ours. I could show you a pretty cageful down here.[2]

It is, I believe, precisely this situation that happened to many of the enthusiastic products of the Catholic revival; for them the world became an end and faith a means. But faith used as a means ceases to be nourished and ceases to be faith. It sounds very well to say that certain human needs are so urgent that we have no time for "prayers and sacraments". But without the prayers and sacraments, our faith starves and dies, and either the means are found to serve the original end or that end is abandoned. Some of those impelled to social activism by the Catholic revival and who fell into this trap substituted secular for religious motivations. But far more people simply "burned out" and abandoned the struggle.

Without the motivations of faith, doing good in the world at considerable personal sacrifice is not something most people can sustain. The Catholic Evidence Guild advised at least an hour in prayer for every hour spent on the platform.

[2] *The Screwtape Letters* (San Francisco: HarperCollins, 2001), pp. 40–43.

Those who kept this counsel were those who stuck with the guild; those who did not, who relied on their own powers, eventually dropped out. Similarly, Mother Teresa and those who worked with her were sustained in their tremendous sacrifices by prayer and the sacraments.

There are, of course, exceptions: "secular saints" who seem sustained by some nonreligious vision or compulsion, but these are exceptions. To motivate ordinary people to self-sacrificing love, they must be put in contact—by prayer and the sacraments—with Self-Sacrificing Love himself, our Lord Jesus Christ. Our priorities must be right. We must not want faith as a means, even a necessary means to doing good. First, we must know God, we must love God, and then we can serve God in our neighbor. "Seek *first* his kingdom and his righteousness, and all these things shall be yours as well" (Mt 6:33, emphasis added). Seek first the other things, and you will lose the Kingdom of Heaven and the other things, too.

The end of the Catholic revival—the Catholic revival of the Wards, the Sheeds, and Chesterton—came when people forgot this truth. The end of the reforms of Vatican II is perilously close at hand because people are forgetting the same truth again. Time after time, great and hopeful movements have been shipwrecked on this rock. But Christianity tells us what to do about such failures: repent and change. Catholic Christianity's version of this formula is to confess your sins, form a firm purpose of amendment, and make reparation for past sins. To help and motivate us in this endeavor, we have the same help we neglected before: prayer and the sacraments.

What is more, we have the Wards, the Sheeds, and Chesterton. For unlike social energy, which comes from group interaction and ceases to exist when the group goes down,

intellectual energy is stored in those marvelous storage bat-
teries called books. We can pick up the book again, see the
vision again, and go out to fight for the vision again. If the
book was written in another age, in another social situation, we may need help in understanding it and applying it
to our times. That is one vital function of scholarship about
men and women such as the Sheeds, the Wards, and
Chesterton.

But the scholar needs to have his priorities very much in
order. Our work is important because the work of those
we try to understand and elucidate is important. And their
work is important because they are trying to understand
and elucidate what God has revealed to us, in nature and
society as well as in scripture. "Therefore every scholar
instructed in the kingdom of God is like a rich man who
brings out of the storehouse things old and new" (Mt 13:52).
And "whoever sets aside one of the commandments, even
the least, and teaches others to do likewise is the least in
the kingdom of heaven, but the one who keeps them and
teaches others to keep them will be accounted in the kingdom of heaven as the greatest" (Mt 5:19).

Scholars and teachers should strive for that kind of greatness, the only kind worth having in the long run, remem
bering that "the one who would be great in the kingdom
of heaven must be the least, and the servant of all" (Mk 9:35)
and also remembering the great servants of God who have
gone before us, William, Wilfrid, and Maisie Ward, Gilbert
Chesterton, and Frank Sheed.

For Further Reading

Rather than simply listing well-known classics in the field, I have chosen six of my favorite authors and listed some books by them. In every case, if you like one book by the author listed, go on to read other books by that author. Some of them, like Chesterton, have over fifty books; even the less prolific authors have a number of other titles. Chesterton and Lewis were largely before my time. Frank Sheed and Peter Kreeft were and are friends of mine, and J.R. Lucas and Richard Swinburne are colleagues in philosophy whom I met at meetings of philosophers. Lucas and Swinburne are a bit more "advanced" or "professional" than some of the others, but both are good writers and will repay the effort of understanding them.

All of the people on the list of "Important Books on Philosophy of Religion" are theists who believe that God exists, but they give good accounts of objections to theistic views before answering them. The only nontheistic philosopher who has written a philosophy of religion and given a fair account of what Christians believe is Antony Flew, who fairly recently acknowledged that God does exist. I am not sure what arguments he would still defend, and therefore I have left his earlier books off of the list of important readings. (Flew has published a new book, *There Is a God*,[1] which gives reasons for rejecting atheism and his openness to religious ideas.) All but one of the books listed under "Books of Readings" include papers by me, and I have listed my own books that are relevant to the subject.

Important Books on Philosophy of Religion

Chesterton, G. K. *The Everlasting Man.* San Francisco: Ignatius Press, 1986.

———. *Orthodoxy.* San Francisco: Ignatius Press, 1986.

Kreeft, Peter. *Heaven: The Heart's Deepest Longing.* San Francisco: Ignatius Press, 1989.

———. *Love Is Stronger than Death.* San Francisco: Ignatius Press, 1992.

Lewis, C. S. *The Abolition of Man.* San Francisco: HarperOne, 2007.

———. *Mere Christianity.* San Francisco: HarperOne, 2007.

———. *Miracles.* San Francisco: HarperOne, 2007.

———. *The Problem of Pain.* San Francisco: HarperOne, 2007.

Lucas, J. R. *The Freedom of the Will.* Oxford: Oxford University Press, 1970.

———. *Freedom and Grace.* London: SPCK, 1976.

Sheed, Frank. *A Map of Life.* San Francisco: Ignatius Press, 1994.

———. *Theology and Sanity.* San Francisco: Ignatius Press, 1993.

Swinburne, Richard. *The Coherence of Theism.* Oxford: Oxford University Press, 1974.

———. *The Existence of God.* Oxford: Oxford University Press, 1979.

[1] New York: HarperOne, 2007.

Books of Readings

Geivett, Douglas, and Gary Habermas, eds. *In Defense of Miracles*. Downers Grove: InterVarsity Press, 1997.

Peterson, Michael, William Hasker, Bruce Reichenbach, and David Basinger, eds. *Philosophy of Religion: Selected Readings*. New York: Oxford University Press, 2006.

Pojman, Louis P., ed. *Philosophy of Religion: An Anthology*. Belmont: Wadsworth Publishing, 2002.

Stewart, Melville, ed. *Philosophy of Religion: An Anthology of Contemporary Readings*. Boston: Jones and Bartlett, 1996.

Swinburne, Richard, ed. *Miracles*. New York: Macmillan, 1989.

Related Works by Richard Purtill

Purtill, Richard. *C. S. Lewis' Case for the Christian Faith*. San Francisco: Ignatius Press, 2004.

———. *A Logical Introduction to Philosophy*. Englewood Cliffs: Prentice Hall, 1981.

———. *Moral Dilemmas*. Belmont: Wadsworth Publishing, 1985.

———. *Thinking About Religion*. Englewood Cliffs: Prentice Hall, 1978.

For more information on these and other works by Richard Purtill, please visit his official Website at www.alivingdog.com/Richard_Purtill.html.

Index